John, Wishing you a happy Birthday

Love Ann.

10.5.48.

Silver Wedding

A portrait of the King and Queen specially taken for the Silver Wedding.

SILVER WEDDING

The Record of
Twenty-five Royal Years

By

LOUIS WULFF, M.V.O.

Author of
"Queen of To-morrow"

London :
SAMPSON LOW, MARSTON & COMPANY, LIMITED

When the Princesses were young: a happy family group.

ACKNOWLEDGMENTS

Thanks are due to P. K. Hodgson, C.M.G., C.V.O., O.B.E., for his courtesy in lending some pictures.

Acknowledgments are due to the following for their help in illustrating this book :

P.A. Reuters—Photos

The Times

Central Press Photos, Ltd.

Graphic Photo Union

Planet News, Ltd.

Marcus Adams

Studio Lisa

Evening News

Imperial War Museum

Bertram Park

Portraits by Dorothy Wilding, London.

FOREWORD

Twenty-five years is a long period in the span of a married couple. To reach the Silver Anniversary together is to have lived a lifetime with each other, to have grown to know each other as well as human beings may, to have shared adventures, hopes, joys, fears and disappointments : and when the marriage is a Royal marriage, and the golden light of the Crown gleams on the silver, it is twenty-five years of history on which husband and wife look back, twenty-five years of history which they themselves have, in some measure, helped to write. Since that Spring morning of 1923, when the young Duke of York led his lovely, smiling Duchess out of Westminster Abbey to be greeted by the cheering crowds of London, what a flood of history has poured through the arches of the years ! As events of national and world importance, grave, gay, ominous or promising, have succeeded each other with lightning change, The King and Queen have remained firm and unchanged, secure in the affections of their peoples, confident in their love for, and finding their happiness with, each other and their children. Theirs is indeed a happy marriage, happy for themselves, and happy for the great family of nations of which they are the head. From every member of that great widespread family, of whatever race, colour or creed, best wishes for health and happiness go in their Silver Wedding Year to the Sovereign and his Consort, to the man and woman who in their private family life set for all the same high example as in their public life together.

L. W.

East Horsley,
February, 1948.

Where the King and Queen spend some of their happiest days: A family group in the grounds of Royal Lodge, Windsor.

CONTENTS

CHAPTER ONE

The Empire's Family

AT first sight, the silver wedding of the Sovereign and his Consort does not seem of any especial significance in the life of a nation, nor does it present itself superficially as an occasion for national rejoicing. A wedding anniversary, unlike the anniversary of a coronation, is something personal, something which pertains to the family life of the monarch, and which has little connection with the performance of his public duties or his attention to matters of State. In a sense, it is more personal than his birthday anniversary, for this is marked invariably by the bestowal of public honours to leading figures of the nation, and, traditionally, by a ceremonial parade of the Brigade of Guards, though it is true that by custom these celebrations are held in June, even when, as in the case of his present Majesty, the actual birthday falls in December. Royal wedding anniversaries, by contrast, pass generally with little public notice, and with no public ceremonies.

Yet the fact that King George the Sixth and his Queen Consort Elizabeth are celebrating their Silver Wedding in this, the twelfth year of their reign, has caught the public imagination and stirred nation- and empire-wide enthusiasm in a way that no other Royal anniversary has done since the Silver Jubilee of King George V.

Behind this apparent contradiction lies an explanation that is important because it lies at the core of the modern British concept of monarchy, and goes some way to show why, in a world of tottering or fallen thrones, the British throne is to-day more firmly established than ever. It is simply that the idea of the family has become an integral part of the idea of monarchy. Laying down the Crown whose unshared weight he found too heavy to bear, the Duke of Windsor said in his farewell broadcast that his brother, the new King, had the " matchless blessing " of a happy home with his wife and children.

In Britain and in the British Commonwealth, comparatively few duties are laid on the King by the constitution or defined by statute. The manifold tasks and duties which make the life of the sovereign a round of almost uninterrupted occupation with affairs have, to a very

*The King and Queen ride in state: escorted by Yeomen of the
Guard with halberds.*

large extent, accumulated by custom, and by the extension by each
succeeding sovereign in turn, since Queen Victoria, of the range and
sphere of Royal activities, until, to-day, the King and Queen share in
every aspect of national life. This is particularly true of that wide
section of Royal duties concerned, not with affairs of State and the
workings of the constitution and the intricacies of Parliamentary
Government, but with direct contact with the King's people, provincial
visits, factory inspections, the opening of new buildings and hospitals,
and bridges and reservoirs. A great part of these duties, essential in
the life of a monarch of modern times, could not be carried out without
a consort. A bachelor King, or an unmarried Queen Regnant, would
be placed in a position of constant difficulty, and it is not easy to see how
in those circumstances the work of the Sovereign could go on without
considerable modification.

In modern days, the King no longer commands the allegiance of
his subjects by leading them, with sword in hand, personally into
battle, but earns their love and adherence by example. To set example
to a family-loving nation is a well-nigh impossible task for a Sovereign

THE EMPIRE'S FAMILY

without a family. That is why one of the King's great strengths lies in the fact that he is, above all things, a family man. That is why such tremendous rejoicing rang through the Empire when Princess Elizabeth, the Heiress Presumptive, married and began a family life of her own. And that is why the celebration of twenty-five years of happy married life by the King and Queen gives everyone in the Empire legitimate cause to share in Their Majesties' private happiness.

To many a famous statesman, just as to unknown clerks and factory workers, the quiet hours he spends with his wife, talking over family affairs, with the grave problems of the day put for a brief space aside, are his greatest source of rest and refreshment, without which he could not continue. Who can doubt that, deprived of the care and loving support of that gracious lady Mrs. Clementine Churchill, her famous husband Winston would have found the heat and burden of the long war days heavier by an almost intolerable amount : or that Field Marshal Smuts, that man of great and optimistic vision, could have enjoyed and endured his life of adventure half as well without the lifelong companionship of his much loved wife, Sibella?

The same is true of the King, though for a king to lay aside completely the trappings of his office is far more difficult than for the most famous or hardest-pressed of statesmen. It is by that very much more that his family circle becomes for him the only place in the world where he may fully relax, forget for the nonce his kingship, and be as other men.

It has been the King's good fortune to find in Her Majesty Queen Elizabeth the ideal partner. Theirs is a marriage of rare happiness. To-day, the affection between them, strengthened by the passing years, and by sorrows, trials and joys shared together, is as plain and easy to see as on that spring day twenty-five years ago when the young fair-haired Duke of York led his smiling radiant bride down the red-carpeted aisle of Westminster Abbey, the same aisle down which, only a few months ago, their daughter, Princess Elizabeth, walked at the side of the man she married for love. To see Their Majesties together, moving perhaps slowly along a

Driving down the course ; Their Majesties arrive at Ascot.

*A wartime group: in the forecourt of Buckingham Palace with
Queen Wilhelmina of the Netherlands.*

double line of bowing and curtsying guests at a State reception at
Buckingham Palace, the Queen regally lovely in one of those jewel
encrusted *robes-de-style* she wears so well, the King in evening clothes,
with the broad blue ribbon of the Garter : or walking with equal ease
of manner between the humming machines of some factory, while men
and women tending them cheer with smiling faces, and wave flags
and coloured streamers, is to see two people completely happy in each
other's company, with such mutual understanding and sympathy
that their words and actions fit into a spontaneously complementary
pattern.

Even were they not the King and Queen, this quality of unison
that marks their every appearance together, so that neither reflects,
but each reciprocates, the actions of the other, would focus
admiring and envying attention upon them as a couple who have
achieved a seldom-found balance of living that can be based only
on the deepest esteem, affection and love. That this happy pair are
the King and Queen of England makes their happiness of much
wider significance. Sanctity of family life, the family as the unit on
which the nation and the state are built, are twin concepts of prime
importance to the democratic outlook. Their denial is the foundation
of the totalitarian system. To see on the Throne a family secure in
deep-seated love and abiding affection gives all other families, rich or

poor, large or small, a sense of added security, and strengthens not merely the great constitutional bonds of imperial unity, but the myriads of family ties from which the strength of the whole nation and commonwealth derives.

In the private lives of the King and Queen away from the public gaze, in their own plainly-furnished apartments at Buckingham Palace, at Royal Lodge, their much-loved home in Windsor Great Park, at Sandringham and at Balmoral, the same happy atmosphere persists. Men and women who have been in the Royal service since long before the Accession cannot recall a major disagreement between the King and Queen. That is not to say that the King and Queen invariably see eye to eye over everything. They are human beings, not fairy-book characters, and it has not been unknown for the King to look somewhat pointedly at the clock, and to exhibit other masculine signs of impatience when the Queen, who sometimes allows her deep interest in people to outweigh her sense of time, has held up the Royal party perhaps ten or fifteen minutes behind their timetable as she talks over war experiences, or rationing difficulties or some other subject of mutual interest with women at a factory bench, or housewives in a new estate.

At such times, the Queen, rejoining the King, will enquire, with her most disarming smile, " Are we a little behind time ? ", at which the King smiles, too, and the party moves off. But however far adrift on their tightly-packed schedule Their Majesties may, on occasion, fall, they never, even though it means cutting short the scant periods of rest allowed in their programme, make up time by omitting any arranged call or visit. The contrary is quite often the case when, in the course of visiting a civic centre or a factory, they hear of some other place of interest or new development nearby which they would like to see. This happened several times during the Royal visit to South Africa in 1947, when the exact timetable of the White Train—as the luxurious Royal train specially built in England for the journey to the order of the South African Railways was known—was liable to be upset if on some small wayside station the King or the Queen caught sight of even a small crowd of onlookers, many of whom had probably ridden or driven scores of miles to see the Royal visitors. A Royal order for an impromptu halt would be given, and while railway officials fussed a little impatiently, thinking of their carefully planned timing, the King and Queen and the two Princesses would alight to talk on the platform with the delighted South Africans. Punctuality is proverbially the politeness of Princes, but both the King and the Queen take the

The King discusses problems with a miner.

deeper view that timetables were made for people, and not people for timetables.

The necessary shortness of Royal visits, many of which have to be dovetailed into a single day's stay in a given area, is sometimes the cause of concern to the Queen, who will often bring her talk with some conducting official or housewife she has met to a close with the remark, "Well, we must go along now. What a pity the time is so short". And the Queen has such sincerity in her voice and her expression that she leaves no doubt at all in the minds of her hearers that she *is* genuinely sorry to leave them.

In Britain, where the movements of the Royal train have to be fitted into so much more elaborate and intricate a general timetable than was the case in South Africa, Their Majesties, however far the programme may have gone adrift during the day, never allow themselves to be late at the station. They cannot "miss" their train, for the Royal train may not leave without its passengers, but they know very well that delay on the Royal special train may easily upset the general working of the railway operations schedule over a wide area, with consequent irritation and annoyance to perhaps hundreds of other travellers.

That is one more of the many little-known ways in which the King and Queen put into practical effect their thoughtfulness and consideration for others.

Another way in which Their Majesties unconsciously reveal their fond affection for each other is to be seen at almost any public function at which they are present together, from the State Opening of Parliament with its elaborate ritual and ceremony, to an affair of minor importance like the opening of a new pumping station on the Sandringham estate. If it is the King who is taking the leading part in the ceremony, or making a speech, the Queen will sit at ease, content to number herself as one of the audience, only occasionally glancing over to her husband. If her eye catches his, a smile of mutual confidence and understanding passes between them. No one who has met and talked with the Queen can fail to be conscious of the sympathy and encouragement that radiate naturally from her, even to complete strangers who are presented to her. All the more is this so in the case of the King. Though to-day His Majesty speaks with confidence when addressing an audience in public or through the microphone in his study when he is delivering his Christmas Day broadcasts, at the beginning of his reign and in his days as Duke of York, public orations were always something of an ordeal for him. It is no secret that the friendly encouragement of his wife's presence, her reassuring smile, did much to help him overcome and master the nervousness that then handicapped him in his public appearances.

Often it must be that the chief performer in a scene cannot himself absorb all the details as readily as another present, but less actively concerned. In this way the Queen frequently plays a considerable part in transforming a somewhat dull, routine ceremony, into another opportunity for warm human contact between the King and his people. With a really remarkable gift for dealing with such situations, the Queen never fails to take in all the details of what is going on while the King's attention is concentrated on the immediate business in hand. Then, when the formal proceedings are at an end, Her Majesty will call to the King's notice a group of wounded ex-servicemen, or some other cluster of people with a special interest, whom she has picked out, and, walking past their waiting car, the King and Queen will cross over to talk with these surprised and delighted folk in that utterly informal, friendly manner that they have made their own. Such an incident occurred soon after the Royal party arrived in Cape Town at the beginning of their great tour of South Africa : and it had more than a little to do with the instant stamping of the seal of success on the Royal visit.

Colonel the Princess Elizabeth rides behind her father on his birthday parade.

His four sons riding with King George V at Windsor.

Their Majesties in full Garter robes at a Chapter of the Most Noble Order at Windsor.

On the big Grand Parade, an imposing white dais had been erected, surmounted by the Royal Arms, hung with flags and decorated with flowers. Here the Administrator of the Cape Province, the Hon. J. G. Carinus, read an address of welcome to Their Majesties, followed by the Mayor of Cape Town, Mr. A. Bloomberg, who also read an address of welcome on behalf of the citizens of Cape Town. The King, in white tropical naval uniform, read a reply to both addresses, while the Queen and the Princesses watched the scene. It was a day of real Cape sunshine, with the temperature something like a hundred in the shade—and the Royal dais was certainly not in the shade. Before the addresses, there were presentations, members of the Cape Province Executive Committee and of the Provincial Council, Mayors of near-by towns, representatives of the South African magistrates, police, railway officials, and others, and their wives, all of whom had to shake hands in turn with the King, the Queen, Princess Elizabeth and Princess Margaret. Thirty-nine minutes were allowed on the official programme for the ceremony, and at the end of that time, everyone, including the Royal party, was feeling the heat, and the earlier excitement and enthusiasm began to wane a little. The King and Queen walked down the steps of the dais to their car. The Queen paused, turned to speak to the King, and both walked across the sun-baked roadway to where a party of war-wounded sat in invalid chairs. South African police and officials, unused to the democratic ways of the Royal family whom they had only just met, were worried as the crowd swallowed up the four Royal visitors, cutting them off from ladies-in-waiting and equerries. For nearly a quarter of an hour, the King and Queen stood there in the blaze of the sun talking to the wounded and to hundreds of other men and women who crowded round them. As they made their way back to their car, the volume of cheering that went up from the whole of the vast crowd was an omen and foretaste of the affection the Royal visitors were to inspire wherever they went in the Union.

That comparatively small incident, which would have passed in this country without attracting much comment, so used are we to the friendly ways of our Royal family, set the whole of Cape Town talking. News of it spread throughout the Union. It was important because it showed the people of South Africa what no amount of speeches and newspaper stories could tell them, that the King and Queen are people of deep human feelings who, when occasion demands, observe ceremonial with punctilious strictness, yet know when to break with formality and how to mingle with a crowd without losing an iota of their dignity.

On that occasion, it was the Queen who took the lead, as on many others. Her Majesty naturally has more opportunities of starting such impromptu breaks from the set programme, because, at most public functions, it is the King who must carry out the majority of the official ceremonies. But there are times when the roles are reversed, and then it is the King who suggests some variation to the Queen with equally happy results.

Princess Elizabeth and Princess Margaret, who are both young women with views of their own, and independent spirits, probably often had ideas for the alteration and improvement of some of the more humdrum functions of the South African tour, which was the first occasion on which they had appeared continuously in public with their parents over such a long period. But such

The King shakes hands with a native Paramount Chief.

ideas, if they were present, were kept strictly to themselves. The Royal sisters kept themselves as well as their ideas quietly in the background to leave the focus of interest always on the King and Queen. This they did with such naturalness and grace that at the start of the tour, the impression was created among a good many South Africans that both the Princesses were more than a little shy. As they became better known this impression soon wore off and the South Africans, whose national tradition is built so closely round the life of the family, recognised and paid tribute to the fine family feeling and splendid upbringing that kept the two young Royal ladies from obtruding themselves in any way.

What the King himself thinks of marriage and family life is best illustrated by his own words. Three months after his marriage, addressing a hospital audience in Liverpool, he referred for the first time in a public speech to his wife. " The Duchess and I ", said the then Duke of York, and his audience caught a gleam of proud affection in his eye as he glanced at his young wife, sitting at his side, " the Duchess and I wish the hospital, its staff and this extension, every prosperity." After that, his references to the Duchess were frequent. At Forfar, the small Scottish town near which is Glamis, the Queen's ancestral home, when he was made a freeman of the Burgh, the Duke claimed to receive the honour " by matrimony ". " I am a very lucky man to have a Scotswoman to share my life " he told guests at an Edinburgh luncheon to celebrate the Silver Jubilee of King George V, and that was no empty oratorical compliment.

Years later, in his first message as King to Parliament, and through them, to his people everywhere, he affirmed this resolve : " It will be my constant endeavour, with God's help, supported as I shall be by my dear wife, to uphold the honour of the realm and promote the happiness of my people." And the support given by the Queen has been an essential factor in the daily life of the King, at peace and in war, ever since. When his elder daughter was about to be married, the King again spoke with deep feeling on the subject of marriage and family life. Replying to the congratulations of the Archbishop of Canterbury and the Bishops and Clergy of the Diocese, he uttered these words : " Those who, like the Queen and myself, have been happy in their married life, know what a bulwark domestic happiness can be. We wish for our daughter and her husband no less happiness than it has been our privilege to enjoy."

Few men could speak more highly in praise of matrimony or pay higher tribute to their partner in the twenty-fifth year of their married life.

The King and Queen pay a call to inspect Army married quarters.

The King's deep sincerity as he spoke touched all his hearers, from the Primate to the youngest of his clergy, as they stood in the Throne Room at Buckingham Palace a few days before Princess Elizabeth's wedding. The Queen, as she listened, was touched, too. A vista of memories, of her own wedding day with all its pomp and crowds, of the anniversaries since, some marked with gaiety in the happy days of peace, some sombered by the gloom of war, but all infused with the happiness of family contentment, must have passed through her mind, and tears were not far from her eyes, tears not of sadness, but of emotion and thankfulness.

The Duke of York and Lady Elizabeth Bowes-Lyon. Their engagement picture.

CHAPTER TWO

Twenty-Five Years Ago

THURSDAY, April 26, in the year nineteen twenty three, dawned with grey skies and light spring rain. Londoners and thousands of visitors to the capital who had come to see the wedding of the young Prince who was second in succession to the Throne of Britain sighed as they looked at the unpromising skies, donned coats and mackintoshes, and set out to pick vantage spots along the Royal routes. Half past eleven was the hour chosen for the wedding service at Westminster Abbey, and in those days, when life ran at a more leisurely pace, the line of men and women watchers was still only three or four deep when ten o'clock struck. An hour later, the crowd had grown to a packed mass extending all the way from Buckingham Palace to the Abbey. It was a cheerful, happy crowd, as London crowds are always apt to be.

From the tall windows of his room on the second floor of Buckingham Palace, the Duke of York, slim, and in those days, still more than a little shy, glanced out at the crowds as he put on his wedding clothes, the colourful light-blue full-dress uniform of a Group-Captain of the Royal Air Force, then a mere infant service, with only five short years behind it. Across his blue tunic was the deeper blue ribbon of the Order of the Garter, with the Garter Star. He wore, too, the star of the second order of British Chivalry, the Ancient Order of the Thistle, which his father, the King, had just conferred on him in compliment to the country of his Scottish bride, the gold aiguillettes of a Personal Aide-de-Camp to the King, and a single row of medals, with the three Service awards of the 1914-18 war proudly among them. As he looked down, along the Mall and across St. James's Park, " His Royal Highness the Bridegroom ", as he was described in the wedding ceremonial programmes, could see the tall figures of his father's Guardsmen lining the route, their scarlet tunics hidden under grey greatcoats, but their tall bearskins proclaiming their peacetime uniforms. Across the Green Park, to the north he could look towards Mayfair, where, in an unpretentious house that was her father's London home, No. 17 Bruton Street, his bride was preparing for the ceremony.

The King and Queen re-visit St. Paul's Walden, where they became engaged.

Along Piccadilly, from Hyde Park Corner to St. James's Street, as on every other part of the processional route, houses were decked with flags, with streamers and with gay coloured bunting. Some streets were "officially" decorated by Westminster City Council. Even the lamp-posts were silver with aluminium paint in honour of the day, and where official decorations ended, private decorations continued, for though there were one million three hundred thousand unemployed in the country, the dreary word austerity had not yet impinged on the nation's consciousness, and the celebration of a Royal wedding was something to be celebrated royally.

It was around Bruton Street and in Piccadilly that the early crowds were thickest, for though it was the bridegroom whose father was the King, and the bride a commoner, with only the courtesy title of "Lady" as an Earl's daughter, it was the bride whom the crowds, especially the women, wanted most to see. Soon they saw her.

Punctually at twelve minutes past eleven, Lady Elizabeth Bowes-Lyon, her cheeks flushed with happiness, her whole being radiant, came out on the arm of her tall father, the Earl of Strathmore and Kinghorne, and entered the waiting carriage. The escort to lead her through the crowd-filled streets to the great grey Church of St. Peter that is the national shrine of Britain, wore, not the scarlet tunics and glittering breastplates of the Life Guards, but the sober workaday blue of the Metropolitan Police, for Lady Elizabeth was not yet a member of the Royal family. For the last time she was journeying through London, that London whose every quarter she was to come to know so well in the years ahead, as a commoner, though the commoner honoured above all others by the choice of the King's son.

So, nearly a quarter of a century later, when her own daughter, Elizabeth, Princess of Great Britain, followed her mother to the same altar of Westminster Abbey, police, and not the Household Cavalry, provided the escort for her bridegroom, and the Duke of Edinburgh drove from Kensington Palace to the Abbey behind four mounted police, though the passing years had transformed their mounts into motor-cycles, and he and his best man rode in a motor-car.

As Lady Elizabeth emerged into the soft daylight of a spring day, a cloak of white ermine over her bridal gown, a wonderful veil of beautiful old lace, lent her by Queen Mary, draped over her soft black hair like a cap, its length falling behind into a long train, she paused for a moment on the arm of her father, who was in the silver-laced uniform of a Lord-Lieutenant. The waiting crowd cheered, and the young bride, to whom the prospect of taking part for the first time as the central figure in a Royal occasion of national importance must have been more than a little intimidating, looked at them with her clear blue eyes—and smiled. As she took her place in the carriage, and the little procession drove off, everyone in the crowd was smiling, too, for her smile was so sincere and infectious with happiness that it warmed the hearts of all. It was the same smile of real happiness that has won her, since, first as Duchess of York, and then as Queen, so many millions of hearts all over the world.

Meanwhile, at Buckingham Palace, the Royal processions to the Abbey had been leaving to the accompaniment of massed cheering. First King George V, in the full dress uniform of an Admiral of the Fleet, with Queen Mary, upright and regal at his side, wearing a superb gown of aquamarine blue and silver, with a lace overdress sparkling with blue crystals, a turban shaped hat of blue and silver, and magnificent diamond ornaments, drove out in a State coach, with a Sovereign's Escort of the Life Guards. Long scarlet cloaks, worn against the drizzle of rain that fell as the King's procession left, hid their gleaming breastplates and scarlet tunics.

Five minutes later, a second State coach swung through the Palace gates, with a Captain's Escort of Life Guards. In it sat the bridegroom, a little pale, but smiling and bowing to the cheers. With him were his two supporters, his brothers, the Prince of Wales—now Duke of Windsor—in the scarlet of the Grenadier Guards, and Prince Henry—

not yet Duke of Gloucester—in the uniform of the Tenth Hussars. His third brother, Prince George, the late Duke of Kent, then still a naval cadet, had gone with his parents.

But it is the procession that had already passed to the Abbey from Marlborough House that gives us to-day a sense of history as we look back across the years. In a gilt coach, drawn by caparisoned horses, and escorted by Life Guards, sat two ladies, strongly alike in looks and bearing. One was Queen Alexandra, still lovely of countenance, despite her seventy-eight years. Wearing a queenly gown of deep violet and gold, she gracefully acknowledged the warm cheers of the crowds who loved her so well. At her side was her sister, Marie, Dowager Empress of All the Russias, whose very title sounds now like an echo of the long-past.

Within the high-roofed Abbey, whose stained windows have patterned so many of the greatest, most splendid, and most solemn scenes in the long pageant of Britain, there is always a sense of history, even on days of no great import, a sense that is deepened and strengthened a thousandfold on the momentous day of a Royal wedding. To those who, like the King and Queen themselves, bridegroom and bride in that earlier ceremony, were present both then and at the wedding of Princess Elizabeth and the Duke of Edinburgh, the twenty-four and a half intervening years seemed in November 1947, to stretch far back into a different world, a world that is already history ; for in contrast to the sombre morning clothes and the plain Service dress of the Royal wedding of 1947, full-dress uniforms of brilliant scarlets and blues and greens and gold and silver, adorned with glittering stars and gleaming orders filled the nave and the chancel with colour and pageantry at the wedding of the Duke and Duchess of York.

By the King's thoughtful dispensation, men guests at the wedding of Princess Elizabeth could come, if they wished, in lounge suits, since, with clothing strictly rationed, to expect the purchase of morning clothes for one day's ceremony would be unreasonable. Such a dispensation at the wedding of the then Duke of York would have been unthinkable. Ambassadors wore full diplomatic uniform ; members of the Cabinet, the Prime Minister, Mr. Bonar Law, among them, were in the dark blue and gold of Privy Councillors: so was Mr. Lloyd George, with his own former chief, Mr. Asquith (later Lord Oxford) in the equally magnificent uniform of the Elder Brethren of Trinity House : and the few men guests who had no uniform to wear hid the plainness of their frock- or morning-coats behind the colourful splendour of their fellows. Even the thirty factory boys, representing the great

The Duke and Duchess take their marriage vows.

industries of Britain, invited to his wedding by the Duke of York as President of the Industrial Welfare Society, had each a new suit for the occasion.

But, if the circumstances and outward appearances were different, the spirit and the inward significance of the ceremony were the same. The Duke of York and his bride were married, as were Princess Elizabeth and the Duke of Edinburgh, according to the form of marriage prescribed for the Church of England, that sacrament which, as the Archbishop of York reminded the Princess and her bridegroom, is, in essentials, the same for cottager and for King. On that April morning in 1923, the Archbishop of Canterbury, Dr. Davidson, repeated the old familiar words of the marriage service. In his clear voice he asked "Albert Frederick Arthur George" if he would have "this woman" to his wedded wife, and "Elizabeth Angela Marguerite" if she would have "this man" to her wedded husband; just as another Archbishop of Canterbury, Dr. Fisher, asked, on a November morning of 1947, "Elizabeth Alexandra Mary" and "Philip" the same questions.

The Royal Marriage Certificate: signed with many famous names.

PAGE 60B

3. Marriage solemnized at *Westminster Abbey* in the *Close* of *St. Peter Westminster* in the County of *Middlesex*

When Married.	Name and Surname.	Age.	Condition.	Rank or Profession.	Residence at the time of Marriage.	Father's Name and Surname.	Rank or Profession of Fat
26th April 1923	Albert Frederick Arthur George Windsor	27 Years	Bachelor	Prince of the United Kingdom of Great Britain and Ireland Duke of York K.G. G.C.V.O. K.T.	Buckingham Palace	George Frederick Ernest Albert Windsor	H. M. King George V. United Kingdom of Great and Ireland and of the Dominions beyond the of the British Empire of Fourteenth Earl of
	Elizabeth Angela Marguerite Bowes-Lyon	22 Years	Spinster	————	17 Bruton Street W.	Claude George Bowes-Lyon	Strathmore and King

ried in *Westminster Abbey* according to the Rites and Ceremonies of the *Established Church* by *Special License*

Marriage solemnized between us:— *Albert* *Elizabeth Bowes Lyon*

e presence of us:—

For in this most solemn moment, rank does not exist, " high and puissant Princes " are equal with their subjects in the sight of God.

So, too, was there a reminiscent ring about the Archbishop of York's address to Princess Elizabeth and the Duke of Edinburgh to those who had heard his predecessor's words to the Royal groom and bride of an earlier day. The present Archbishop, Dr. Garbett, was, as Bishop of Southwark, himself present at the wedding of Their Majesties.

In words that now seem almost to have a ring of prophecy about them, the venerable Archbishop Dr. Lang—who was afterwards to crown the couple then before him—standing before the Altar in his white cope, told the Duke of York and his newly married Duchess, " The nations and classes which make up our commonwealth too often live their lives apart. It is therefore a great thing that there should be in our midst one family which, regarded by all as in a true sense their own, makes the whole Empire kin, and helps to give to it the spirit of one family life. It is your privilege to be members of that family and that central home.

" You cannot resolve that your wedded life shall be happy," he told the Royal pair. " But you can and will resolve that it shall be noble. You will think not so much of enjoyment as of achievement. You will have a great ambition to make this one life now given to you something rich and true and beautiful. And you will, we are assured, resolve to make this wedded life of yours a blessing not only to yourselves but to others, not least to those who in a world of toil and struggle have most need of help and cheer. The warm and generous heart of this people takes you to-day into itself. Will you not in response take that heart, with all its joys and sorrows, into your own ? "

How fully and in what splendid measure have the King and Queen fulfilled the words of that wise churchman of twenty-five years ago !

Other words of the Archbishop brought for the first time the mention of factories and workers within them to a Royal wedding. " You, sir," he said to the Duke, " have given many proofs of your care for the welfare of our working people. You have made yourself at home in their mines, and shipyards and factories. You have brought the boys of the workshop and the public school together in free and frank companionship. You have done much to show your own sense and to increase the public sense of the honour and dignity of labour."

To the Duchess, the Archbishop said, " And you, dear bride, in your

Buckingham Palace balcony : April 26th, 1923.

old Scottish home, have grown up from childhood with country folk, and friendship with them has been your native air. So have you both been fitted for your place in the people's life."

Two incidents of that Royal wedding left a lasting impression on all who saw them, for each was a pointer to the character of the two principal actors in the scene. The first was when the Duke of York, waiting patiently at the altar rail, the minutes dragging slowly by, even though his bride was punctual, noticed something amiss with the cushions on which he and she would later kneel. He spoke to his brothers, and the Prince of Wales stepped over to put it straight. To-day, the King still has that same keen eye for detail, that dislike for the smallest thing out of place. The other concerns the bride. As she walked, a fairy-like figure on the arm of her bridegroom towards the Great West Door of the Abbey, she carried on her arm a simple wedding bouquet of white roses—the flower of York. She paused, looked round, and with great deliberation, went forward to the flat tomb of the Unknown Warrior, where she reverently laid down her wedding flowers, in spontaneous tribute to the million dead of the first World War. That was the first of the thousands of occasions, in public and in private, that Her Majesty has shown her unerring sense of what is fitting, her gift for bringing a human touch of warmth to the most formal of ceremonies.

The Queen's wedding dress was, according to the records of the time, one of the simplest ever made for a Royal wedding. It was of chiffon moiré, specially made to the exact old ivory tint required to tone with the veil of Pont de Flandres lace lent her by Queen Mary. It was medieval in style, and Lady Elizabeth showed that sensible disregard of the extremes of fashion that has always been hers by insisting that the waist should be at the normal line, instead of way below it, as was the mode of the day. The bodice was square cut, crossed in front with bands of silver lamé, embroidered with pearls, and a straight band of silver, also richly embroidered, was brought down the full length of the front of the dress. Another band of silver lamé, with the same embroidery, and fringed with pearls, showed through the lace train at the back. There was a triple train effect, the old lace being mounted on tulle, with a longer train of finest Nottingham lace, modelled on the Old Malines pattern, beneath. The bride's choice of machine-made Nottingham lace—her bridesmaids also wore it—was made deliberately with the object of stimulating interest in this particular British manufacture, and is yet another example of the way in which both the King and Queen constantly consider the public and national welfare in even the most personal details of their lives.

Among the wedding presents to the Duke and Duchess were some lovely pieces of jewellery given the bride by King George and Queen Mary, and by her own parents. King George gave his daughter-in-law

Buckingham Palace balcony; November 20th, 1947.

The Duke smiles at his bride.

to be a diamond and turquoise suite, consisting of a tiara, necklace, brooch, earrings, and hair ornaments. Queen Mary gave her diamonds and sapphires, her father, the Earl of Strathmore, a diamond tiara and a rope necklace of diamonds and pearls. Her mother gave her a diamond and pearl necklace and bracelet, and the Duke, her bridegroom, gave her a necklace of the same stones, with a pendant to match. These jewels, of course, remain among the Queen's most treasured possessions to-day.

Treasured, too, by the King to-day is the exquisite miniature of his bride which was a wedding gift to him from the Countess of Strathmore. King George gave his son silver candelabra and a writing table, at which the King worked for many years as Duke of York, and which he still uses now in his study at Royal Lodge.

Like all Royal functions, the wedding of the Duke and Duchess of York was timed to the minute. At 11.7, Queen Alexandra left Marlborough House. A minute later the King and Queen left Buckingham Palace. At 11.12 the bride left her home in Bruton Street. A minute later H.R.H. "the bridegroom" left Buckingham Palace, to reach the Abbey at 11.25, three minutes before the bride, who was due to arrive—and did arrive punctually—at 11.28. two minutes before the service began.

She had eight bridesmaids as did her daughter after her : six chosen from her own friends, and two child attendants. They were Lady Mary Cambridge (who married the Duke of Beaufort later that year), Lady Katharine Hamilton (now Lady Katharine Seymour, and a Woman of the Bedchamber to Her Majesty), Lady Mary Thynne (now Lady Mary Alexander and for ten years Lady of the Bedchamber to Her Majesty), Miss Diamond Hardinge (who died four years later), Lady May Cambridge (now Lady May Abel-Smith) and Miss Betty Cator (who married the Queen's brother, the Hon. Michael Bowes-Lyon five years later), with the Hon. Elizabeth Elphinstone and the Hon. Cecilia

Bowes-Lyon as junior attendants. They wore dresses of ivory coloured chiffon embroidered in a design of leaves, carried out in silver tissue. Leaf-green tulle sashes at the waist were held in place by a white rose and a silver thistle, and they wore a bandeau of silver roses and silver leaves on their heads. Each wore a brooch with the initials " E.A." and a coronet in diamonds in the centre of a rose of York in carved crystal. They were the gift of the bridegroom.

The Duke of York married his bride with a ring of plain gold, made from a nugget found in the Welsh mine near Barmouth. The ring with which the Duke of Edinburgh married Princess Elizabeth was made from the very same nugget of Welsh gold. After the Duke and Duchess were married, the owner of the nugget found there was enough gold left to make another ring. He kept it, with the determination to offer it to the first of their children to marry—and soon after her engagement was announced in July 1947, Princess

" T.R.H. the Bride and Bridegroom" : they have just left the Abbey on their way to Buckingham Palace. Note the entwined " A and E " and the lavish decorations of those days.

Going away 1923. *The Duke and Duchess leave the Palace for Waterloo.*

Elizabeth was offered, and gladly accepted, the gold for her own wedding ring.

From the Abbey, the Duke and Duchess drove through cheering crowds by an extended route to the Palace, a route which, to her own regret, it was not possible for Princess Elizabeth to follow when her wedding day came along. As the newly married Royal pair left the Abbey, the sun, which had been struggling with grey clouds all morning, broke through, to the delight of the crowds, eager for the smiling Duchess to have the traditional happy luck of the bride " whom the sun shines on ".

And fortunate and happy, for twenty-five years, she and her husband have been, though little either of them thought as they left the Abbey on that distant spring day, that their path would lead to the Throne, their happiness be the happiness of the nation and empire.

When Princess Elizabeth was married, all the empire, and, indeed, most of the world, heard her take her marriage vows. Her clear voice came through loudspeakers in countless homes as she uttered the binding words that plighted her troth : " I will ". At the King's own commands, microphones were installed in the Abbey so that the whole of his peoples everywhere might listen, if they wished, to the wedding service of their own future Queen. How many of them did wish is indicated by what happened at a big factory in the East end of London on the Princess's wedding day. The management, thinking the vast majority of their employees were of decidedly left-wing views, made no arrangements for the wedding broadcast to be heard in the factory. An hour before the marriage broadcast began, a deputation of shop-stewards waited on the management to inform them the women workers had unanimously decided to stop work and go home unless they could hear the programme. They heard it.

. No such arrangements were possible at the wedding of the Duke and Duchess of York. All the wireless listeners of those days could hear was an evening broadcast of the wedding anthem " Beloved, let us love one another ", which had been sung while the Royal party were signing the registers in Edward the Confessor's chapel at the Abbey. The Abbey choir, with Mr. Sydney Nicholson, the organist, had special permission from the Dean to visit the BBC studio at Marconi House for the broadcast, and for the rest of the wedding broadcast programme, listeners had to be content with a " Bright Evening " feature of songs, recitations, violin solos, and selections by the band of the Irish Guards.

Another pointer to the difference between the world of that day and ours to-day is the fact that a newspaper reported with some pride that the first aeroplane to leave London for the Irish Free State since its formation in the previous year carried Press photographs of the

Twenty-four years later. Princess Elizabeth and her husband leaving for their honeymoon.

The wedding cake of 1923.
It weighed 900 lbs.

wedding : which is also an illustration of that binding power upon the empire's peoples of Royal marriages of which the Archbishop of York had spoken ; an illustration to be repeated in a different form at the wedding of Princess Elizabeth when two lovely wedding gifts came to her from the people of the (officially) non-Royalist Dominion in the form of Waterford glass and old Irish silver.

On that April day of 1923 the scene in the State Dining Room where the King and Queen, the Bride and Bridegroom, and sixty-two other principal guests sat down at six circular tables decorated with gold plate and pink tulips and white lilac, was a magnificent one, the uniforms of the men and the lovely dresses of the women reflected in the great wall-mirrors, under the soft, flattering light of the wonderful crystal chandeliers hanging from the gold and white ceiling, a scene such as London may not see for many a long day, perhaps never again. The sixty-one other guests sat in the Ball Supper Room. Champagne was served, and King George V rose to give the single wedding toast, " I ask you to drink to the health, long life, and happiness of the bride and bridegroom." This, in accordance with the invariable custom of Royal weddings, was the only speech.

Immediately afterwards, the Duke led his Duchess into the Green Drawing Room, another of the lofty, beautifully proportioned State Apartments on the first floor of the Palace, to cut the cake, a giant affair in four tiers, weighing nine hundred pounds. An RAF string band played in an adjoining room, and the Duchess and her husband cut the first slice of cake. They found some difficulty with the silver knife provided, and the veteran Duke of Connaught, only surviving son of Queen Victoria, had to come to their aid. No such difficulty arose at the wedding of Princess Elizabeth, for following the modern custom, the caterers had made special provision for the first slice to come out at a mere touch.

Perhaps something of the development of the monarchy may be seen if we look first at the Duke and Duchess of York leaving Buckingham Palace for their honeymoon, then at their daughter, Princess Elizabeth, leaving with her husband, the Duke of Edinburgh, on the same happy journey of romance, all but twenty-five years after. As the open landau with its four grey horses waited at the Grand Entrance in the Inner Quadrangle of Buckingham Palace to take the bride and bridegroom of that earlier day to the station, the King, with many of his guests, stood at the Palace doorway to wave goodbye. The three brothers of the bridegroom ran across to the archway that leads to the Palace forecourt, to pelt the pair with confetti from one side, while the bridesmaids did the same from the other, as their carriage passed through. A moment later, a shower of paper rose petals, made by blind workers for the occasion, fell on the bridal carriage. They came from Queen Mary, Princess Mary (now the Princess Royal) and from Princess Victoria, King George V's favourite sister, who

On their honeymoon: a talk after a morning walk.

The Duke and his bride in the grounds of Polesden Lacey.

had gone out onto the Palace balcony for the purpose of the " bombardment."

When Princess Elizabeth and her husband left the Palace in an exactly similar open landau, drawn again by grey horses, the King and Queen, with their guests, were again at the Grand Entrance, watching the couple take their places. This time, it was the King himself who, after a hurried word with the Queen, led the " bombarding party " across the quadrangle, running to cut off the bridal coach before it passed through the arch. Bridesmaids and best man ran too, outpacing the King, and the other Royal guests, Kings and Queens, Princes and Princesses, took eager part in the rush. So did the Queen. Raising her long skirt of gold lamé from the ground, Her Majesty ran with a will across the sanded forecourt, to the surprise and delight of the privileged few watchers in the quadrangle, who had never before seen a King and Queen of England running together, even for a few yards. At the archway, as the Duke of Edinburgh and his smiling Princess came up, everyone in the Royal party flung rose petals—again of paper, made by the blind—into the coach, until bride and groom were covered in the pale pink emblems. Out through the archway went the carriage into the forecourt, where a crowd of some twelve hundred, relatives and friends of members of the Court, awaited it. And with it went the King and Queen and their guests, now falling behind as the horses began to trot. Not until they reached the very gates of the Palace, a yard or two from the packed cheering crowds outside, did the King and Queen halt. They stood there, alone in the gathering darkness of the November afternoon, following their daughter's honeymoon coach with their eyes, as it went proudly down the Mall, past the tall flagstaffs with their long banners of blue, initialled with " E and P " in gold. The other guests, Royal and those of lesser degree, stood back, instinctively withdrawing from the mother and father at this moment of family emotion. And so, for several moments, they stayed, the slim-figured, young-looking man in naval uniform, who is King of England, and his wife, the Garter ribbon a vivid blue against the gold and apricot of her dress, looking, as parents are apt to do when wedding parties break up, a little pensive and reminiscent, remembering perhaps the day of their own wedding, when they, too, had all the world before them . . .

Around the Palace gates, the crowds, more delighted than ever at this totally unexpected close view of their King and Queen, cheered and cheered again. It was a moment such as even London had not seen before, for no other King had walked to the gates of his Palace with his consort on such a day. It was a scene that could happen nowhere outside the British Commonwealth, the Sovereign Head of a great nation and his Queen standing, without guards, in the midst of a vast crowd of their people, yet alone with their thoughts and memories.

With a last lingering look along the Mall, where the wedding coach had now disappeared into the darkness, the King and Queen turned to re-enter the Palace, and, before they had reached the grey-stone building round which so much of their lives together has revolved, they had put off private thoughts and feelings, to don once again the mantle of Royalty that can so rarely be laid aside.

Sea Rangers from Princess Elizabeth's own old company at Windsor had, at the Princess's own request, places of honour in the front of the crowds within the forecourt. The Queen paused to speak to several of them, asking how long they had had to stand, whether they had had a good view of the bride and groom. While she was speaking, the King joined in with a smile, to tell the Queen that she need not worry to ask if they had had food, for he had already found out that provision had been made for this. That may seem a small incident of little import : but it shows the true, unfailing thoughtfulness of both the King and Queen, for most parents, of whatever rank and station, could have been forgiven for omitting all but the most demanding of courtesies at such a time : and this was an act that need not have been done.

The end of the earlier Royal marriage story is easy to tell. From Buckingham Palace, the Duke and Duchess drove through crowded, gaily decorated streets to Waterloo. Even in those early days, the new Duchess gave signs of that never-failing consideration for others that remains one of her most endearing characteristics to-day. Her going-away dress was of soft dove-grey embroidered crepe-romain, with a matching coatee at the back. Over it she wore a travelling coat

of the same shade of crepe marocain (whose length seems to have given a pre-view of the " New Look " of 1948) and with it beige antelope shoes. It was in choosing her going-away hat that the Duchess showed how much she keeps other folks in mind. She insisted on a small hat of brown with an upturned brim and only a small feather mount at the side, so that the crowds whom she knew would wait patiently to see her should not be robbed of their pleasure because fashion dictated a wide-brimmed hat which would obscure her face.

From Waterloo, in a flower-filled train, the Royal couple went to Bookham, whence they drove to Polesden Lacey, the lovely house set in the hills of Surrey, lent them by their friend, Mrs. " Ronnie " Greville for their honeymoon. The house and its spacious, well-laid grounds, were bequeathed to the National Trust by Mrs. Greville on her death in 1942.

That Royal wedding made history in several ways. Westminster Abbey, now regarded as the only fitting setting for the public celebration of a Royal wedding, was not always so considered. The last male member of the Royal Family to be married there before the Duke of York was King Richard III, who married Anne of Bohemia on January 20, 1382. Since the days of that distant monarch the Abbey had no Royal weddings until 1919 when Princess Patricia, daughter of the Duke of Connaught, married Commander (now Admiral Sir Alexander) Ramsay. Just over a year before the Duke's marriage, his sister Princess Mary (now Princess Royal) had married Viscount Lascelles (the late Earl of Harewood) in the Abbey, on February 28, 1922, and the fact that King George chose the Abbey again for the wedding of the first of his sons to marry was taken as an indication that the King realised that the family events of the Royal House of Windsor were, in a wider sense, the family events of all his peoples, to be fittingly celebrated at the family church of the Empire, the historic Abbey within his capital. That wise decision has been taken as a precedent since. Only the wedding of the Duke of Gloucester in 1935 took place away from the Abbey. It had to be held in private in the chapel at Buckingham Palace owing to the death of the Duchess's father.

As the time for Princess Elizabeth's wedding approached suggestions were made that it should be held out of London, perhaps at St. George's Chapel, Windsor, because of the need for austerity. But the King waved all such ideas aside. He knew that, however austere the entertainments connected with it might necessarily have to be, the wedding of the Heiress Presumptive to his Crown was an Empire event of the first magnitude, which could be properly celebrated only in the capital. And, accordingly, the Princess, like her father and mother before her, took her marriage vows at the High Altar of Westminster Abbey.

The Duke and Duchess of York at Balmoral with Queen Mary.

The wedding of the Duke of York was significant in another way. Two and a half centuries had elapsed since a King of England had given his assent to the marriage of a son in the direct line of succession with one of his own subjects. That Prince was James, Duke of York, afterwards James II. In 1923, the principle that Princes and Princesses are free, as are other men and women, to follow the dictates of their own hearts in the choice of a companion for life, was by no means generally recognised. It was true that both Princess " Pat " and Princess Mary had made love matches with men of their choice, but the marriage of a Prince of the Blood Royal was a different matter. Obviously, though Lady Elizabeth Bowes-Lyon could claim a proud descent and Royal lineage from the ancient Kings of Scotland—Robert the Bruce is among her ancestors—the match between her and the King's son could not by the wildest stretch of imagination be regarded as anything in the nature of a marriage of policy. This background fact, coupled with what was known of the two young people, left no shadow of doubt in the public mind that the Duke of York was making a real love match. And the public were not wrong.

Tales are told that the Duke proposed some three times before Lady Elizabeth would accept him. Whether these are strictly true or not, it is certain that the Duke had paid court to his bride for a long time. There is the authority of her father for that statement. Writing to an old family retainer in reply to congratulations on the wedding, the Earl of Strathmore wrote, " His Royal Highness has a high sense of duty and is a fine type of the young Englishman, and has been a devoted suitor for two or three years." The Earl added " We are grieved to lose our daughter who is adored by all our family." He could not know then that his words would still ring true twenty-five years later when Her Majesty the Queen is undoubtedly adored by all her much larger family—the peoples of the Empire.

It was when they were both quite small that the Duke and Duchess first met, but it was not until 1920 when the Duke of York paid a visit to the historic castle of Glamis with his sister Princess Mary, that the two came together. At that time Lady Elizabeth was acting as hostess, harassed by the knowledge that her much loved mother was seriously ill. But she did not allow her private grief to interfere with her duties as hostess, and the Duke went away much impressed by the young daughter of the ancient House of Strathmore.

It was on a Sunday, in January, 1923, that the Duke, who was staying for the weekend as the guest of the Earl and Countess of Strathmore at St. Paul's Walden, their seat in Hertfordshire, went for an afternoon walk in the woods with Lady Elizabeth. They returned to the house an engaged couple. On January 15 the news was given to the world in the Court Circular, the official vehicle for all such announcements. The traditional words ran " It is with the greatest pleasure that the King and Queen announce the betrothal of their beloved son the Duke of York to the Lady Elizabeth Bowes-Lyon, daughter of the Earl and Countess Strathmore and Kinghorne, to which union the King has gladly given his assent "—exactly the same formula as was used by the King to announce Princess Elizabeth's engagement to Prince Philip. Behind the formal phrases of the official announcement lay a deep feeling of happiness on the part of King George V and Queen Mary, who were delighted that their second son should, so early in life, have found an ideal partner—just the same feeling as the King and Queen shared at Princess Elizabeth's choice.

On a State occasion: The Duke in full dress naval uniform wears the Garter. The Duchess wears a tiara with her evening gown.

CHAPTER THREE

Foundations of a Reign

IN the years between 1923 and 1936, the foundations of a new reign were being laid with care and skill, though even the two persons most closely concerned could have no idea of the great destiny for which they were preparing. It has always been the King's way to carry out any task or duty which comes his way with conscientious application, and in the days when he was Duke of York, he applied himself to the different duties of the period with the same painstaking care and thoroughness with which he to-day carries out his high duties as the reigning sovereign. Always at his side was the young Duchess, whose smiling charm and friendly manner made her easily the most popular Princess in the country.

The Royal pair began their married life with White Lodge, a Georgian house in one of the loveliest sites in Richmond Park, as their home. It had long Royal associations, for Queen Mary had spent much of her girlhood there, when it was the home of her mother, the Duchess of Teck. But there was not very much time for the young couple to enjoy the delights of their country home, or indeed, to spend as much time as they would have wished in each other's company, for demands for their appearance at various centres all over the country, requests for their attendance separately or together at functions of all kinds, flowed in at such a rate that scarcely a single day passed without one public engagement, and often three or four functions had to be attended in a day. This experience made the King decide, when Princess Elizabeth married, that a strict limit should for a time be set on the number of functions she and her husband would undertake, so that the first months of their married life should not be spoiled by an overwhelming weight of public engagements.

The busy programme set the Duke and Duchess drove them reluctantly to the conclusion that, much as they both loved the countrified air of Richmond Park, White Lodge was too far from London, involving too much waste of time travelling home to change for evening functions, and they set about looking for a London house. For a time they lived in Curzon House, the very site where a " fortress

Cutting Christmas cake for the wounded of 1914–1918 at a Buckingham Palace party.

flat " was provided for their use in war, should Buckingham Palace have been rendered uninhabitable by the enemy. But for various reasons, this house was not satisfactory, and so it came about that when Princess Elizabeth was born, her parents had no town house of their own, and the baby who was third in succession to the throne, was born in her grandparents' home at 17 Bruton Street. A few months later the Duke and Duchess felt again the clash between private wishes and official duties, this time in a much deeper way. They had to leave for Australia, where King George V had commissioned his second son to open the new Federal Parliament Buildings at Canberra, and this meant leaving their eight-months old daughter behind, for a separation that would last six months.

Before they left, negotiations were in progress for the taking over of 145 Piccadilly, a moderate sized house on Crown property at Hyde Park Corner, as their home, and into that house, which had been got ready for them during their absence, they moved on their return from Australia in June, 1927. For nine and a half years it was to remain their London home, the " Palace with a Number ", the private house over which, on December 11, 1937, the Royal Standard was broken on the first day of the new reign.

" 145 " became the most famous house in London, and one of the strongest magnets for visitors, who would stand for hours on the pavement to catch a glimpse of the Duke and Duchess going in or out, or to see Princess Elizabeth—and later Princess Margaret—being taken for her afternoon outings in the Park as a baby, or playing happily in Hamilton-Gardens, just behind the house, as a little girl.

Inside, the Royal home was furnished with the quiet unostentatious comfort of good taste. There was no attempt at ornateness or over-elaboration. The tall black double front doors opened onto a wide, but not very deep, hall, carpeted in plain moleskin brown. Three steps led up to the morning room, which the Duke used first as his study, later moving to one of the upstairs rooms. On either side of the steps stood two tall tusks of an elephant the Duke himself shot in Uganda. The whole atmosphere of " 145 " was of a comfortable home rather than of the formal residence of a State personage, and if houses can be said to reflect the personalities of those who live in them, " 145 " was certainly a happy, contented house. Across its portal stepped many famous figures, admirals, generals, air marshals, Cabinet Ministers and politicians, Dominion and foreign envoys, and less well-known but important figures from the world of industry, for despite its home-like atmosphere, it was the official residence of the Duke of York, and the Duke was a very busy man. It was the Duke's butler, Mr. Ainslie, tall, quiet, and perfect-mannered, who opened the doors to important visitors, and it is an indication of the trust and affection Their Majesties inspire in those who serve them that to-day Mr. Ainslie is still the King's senior retainer, Steward at Buckingham Palace.

Leaders of industry were frequent among the daily callers, and letters from them were numerous in the morning mail which the Duke would deal with every day without fail at ten a.m. with his secretary. Industry and industrial welfare, then a little-known field, were uppermost among the Duke's interests, and many a scheme of

" *The Palace with a number.*" *Crowds watching for Princess Elizabeth to leave* 145 *Piccadilly.*

The Duke plays golf with Frank Hodges, the Labour M.P.

*The Duke, partnered by Sir Louis Greig, takes a volley
at the Wimbledon championships 1926.*

workers' welfare taken for granted to-day has its origin in suggestions made by the Duke, or in ideas put forward and encouraged by him in those days. He held the post of President of the Industrial Welfare Society, a post he regarded as of considerable importance. There was nothing fashionable or of great popular appeal in the work it involved, nor did the Duke seek for popularity as he went round factories and plants all over the country. Relations between employer and employed were changing, a new attitude of greater humanism was gradually spreading among industrialists, which to the Duke seemed to be of great promise. He well knew what bitterness poor relations between employers and employed could engender. The National Strike was not long over, and though he was, by his constitutional position, debarred from taking any part whatever in that great dispute, he had studied it, the causes underlying it, and the methods used by the authorities for dealing with it. In public, all he could do was to inspect the milk depot in Hyde Park, to see how one vital national service was being maintained. In private he followed the whole course of events with the utmost attention.

All this helped to convince the Duke that anything he could do to foster a better feeling between the two sides of industry would be a real national service, a conviction and purpose in which he had the complete and enthusiastic support of his father, King George V. The Industrial Welfare Society was a tool ready to his hand for this work, and he used it with energy, patience and perseverence. No distance was too great for him to travel to watch some new experiment in better factory conditions : no process was too unpleasant for him to examine. He undertook all these factory visits with a minimum of fuss and ceremony which both endeared him to the men and women he went to see, and enabled him to see factories in their everyday guise, and not as set pieces for a Royal inspection.

Apart from the national benefits which resulted from this new form of Royal visit which brought a Prince to the side of an overalled workgirl, or a grimy and sweating furnace hand, the Duke himself derived advantage from his tours. He learned to know industry from the inside as few, if any, other Princes have known it : he became familiar with the view point of the men at the benches and their foremen, as well as of their employers, knowledge which stood him in wonderful stead when, in the later days, he went as King among his people in the war factories and centres of national production.

Those industrial visits and talks—for the Duke would spend long hours after a factory tour talking over problems with managers and

Colour Plates : Their Majesties the King and Queen.
Portraits by Dorothy Wilding, London.

directors—and his own famous annual holiday camps for public-schoolboys and boys from industry, are two of the foundation stones on which the King has built so firm a structure of universal goodwill during the eleven years of his reign.

" I should not like it to be thought that my interest in the industries

A study that shows the Duchess's charm.

A characteristic study of the Duke.

of our country is confined merely to theoretical and speculative considerations : accordingly I try whenever possible to see the actual working of those theories and thus learn their value by practical experience," he said.

No sketch of the King's earlier days can be complete without some account of the great experiment in industrial relations which he launched without very much fuss in the form of his annual camp. Nothing quite like it had ever been attempted in this country before. The Duke's idea was based, like most of his ideas, on his sound practical knowledge of humanity. He had noticed, both in his days in the Royal Navy, and afterwards, as he went round the country, that social and other distinctions were apt to be obliterated in the field of sport. If boys who would one day be foremen and leaders of their trade unions could mix with boys destined perhaps one day to be managers or owners of industrial undertakings, the resultant knowledge they would each gain of the other's point of view could do nothing but good to themselves and to the future of British industries : and the Duke, with greater foresight than was usually put to his credit, saw quite clearly that the well-being of the country, in peace or war, lay in a sound backbone of industry, unbroken by a succession of strikes and disputes. First at New Romsey then at Southwold, in Suffolk, the Duke invited 200 boys each from industry and from the public schools to be his guests at a fortnight's holiday camp. He paid all expenses out of his own pocket, and spent one night under canvas with the boys each year, joining with vigour in all the camp games and rough-and-tumbles. Many times as he toured war factories or visited his troops in later years, he found men in responsible posts at the benches or on the executive side, commissioned or in the ranks, who greeted him proudly as old campers. Small though the movement had to be, the King has had the satisfaction of knowing that it did much good, that the spirit of goodwill and co-operation which it was designed to promote, permeated far into many fields of industrial endeavour.

But, keen as he was on this side of his duties, there were many other claims on the time and attention of the Duke of York. He was President of the British Empire Exhibition at Wembley in 1925, and put a tremendous amount of work into the organisation of the "University of Empire" as he christened it.

He was President of the British Empire Cancer Campaign, too, and,

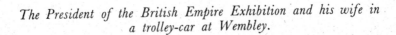

The President of the British Empire Exhibition and his wife in
a trolley-car at Wembley.

Princess Elizabeth christening group. The Duke of Connaught, King George V and the Earl of Strathmore stand with the Duke of York behind the Duchess, sitting with her baby between Queen Mary and the Countess of Strathmore.

incidentally, paid his first official visit to No. 10 Downing Street in this capacity during the days of Mr. Ramsay MacDonald's first Labour Government, to see a Campaign film.

Besides these and many other posts which he held, besides the continuous stream of official visitors at 145 Piccadilly, and the large number of public and ceremonial appearances at Courts and Levées which he, sometimes accompanied by his Duchess and sometimes alone, had to make, there was a great deal of entertaining to be done at home. Even at public functions in those days it was noted that the Duke was more at ease when the Duchess was with him. At home, he and his Duchess, whose smile one American visitor described as " the most welcoming thing in London ", made together an ideal host and hostess. They were, as Princess Elizabeth and the Duke of Edinburgh are to-day, the leading young couple of the Empire, and to their friendly, hospitable table in the simply furnished dining room of 145 Piccadilly, came famous people from all the world over.

About twenty was the usual number for these dinner parties, and, even in those unrationed and non-austerity days of plenty, there was nothing of exaggerated luxury at the Royal table. Neither the King nor the Queen have ever liked ornate display or over-elaboration whether in the dinner menu or in any other form. Their guests at 145 Piccadilly enjoyed excellently cooked simple fare, but it was not merely the quality of the food that made their invitations the most sought after in London. Nor was the explanation entirely in the Royal rank of the host and hostess. (The dignity of a Princess had been bestowed on the Duchess by King George V on her marriage.) It lay rather in the quality and personality of the host and hostess themselves. Well-matched, happy, and making no secret of their deep affection for each other, they made their guests happy without effort. It was—and still is—a pleasure merely to be in their company. After dinner, when the ladies had left the table, the Duke enjoyed serious talk over the affairs of

A happy family study. The Duke and Duchess with the baby Princess Elizabeth.

53

A very early admirer. A war veteran greets three year old Princess Elizabeth.

the day with his guests, who were nearly always well-known folk in their own walks of life, though no narrow distinctions of " Society " ruled their choice. Nearly always they, too, learned something from their host, who had—and still retains—a habit of surprising experts in various fields by his own sound knowledge of their pet subject. Later, when the whole party foregathered in the long, elegantly furnished drawing room on the first floor, the Duchess would complete the happiness of the guests by her own charm. To-day, the Queen is one of the most charming conversationalists in the country. Then, though her experience was the smaller by many full years, her active mind, her wide and thorough knowledge of literature and the arts, her love of the theatre and of music, and above all, her generous and wide human sympathy, made her the subject of universal praise.

When, as happened all too rarely for their own pleasure, the Duke and Duchess had a free night, with neither official engagements nor a private party, they liked to dine quietly together at an early hour and go out privately to a theatre, sitting, as they would still prefer to do, were it possible for the King and Queen, in the stalls and not in a box. Such visits were unheralded and unannounced, and more than once, West-end managers, flurried at the arrival of King George and Queen Mary at the play, found to their surprise, when they looked round the audience, the Duke and Duchess of York sitting almost unnoticed in the stalls. Not to be noticed or fussed over was exactly what the Royal couple most liked, and this was one of the reasons which made it often inconvenient for them to visit the cinema, because of the difficulty of booking seats at short notice without making it an " official " visit. Both are very fond of the films, and occasionally they would slip into one of the West-end cinemas perhaps with two friends, taking their chance of a seat with the rest. Nowadays, of course, the King and Queen go very rarely to the cinema, except on such formal occasions as the annual Royal Film Show, in aid of the

The Duke in full dress uniform as a Group Captain in the R.A.F. with his brother the Duke of Gloucester on their father's birthday parade.

Cinematograph Trade Benevolent Fund, which, like the Royal Variety Show, in aid of the Variety Artistes Benevolent Fund, has now become a regular fixture in the Royal year. It is, incidentally, a misnomer to call either of these events a " Royal Command Performance." Strictly, Command Performances are only those at which the King himself chooses the entertainment, perhaps even nominating the actors or the singers, and to which the audience are invited by the Lord Chamberlain by the King's command. The last such Command Performance in London was held in June 1939, in honour of Monsieur Lebrun, last President of the Third French Republic to visit Britain. It took place at the Royal Opera House, Covent Garden, and all men present in the audience wore uniform or Court dress.

More in the nature of " Command Shows " of modern times, since Their Majesties choose the programme, are the cinema performances which the King and Queen like to see in their own home, at Buckingham Palace, Windsor Castle, Sandringham or Balmoral, each of which is equipped for sound-film projection. Newest British, and in normal times, American, films are seen by the King and Queen often before they have been released for public showing. Full payment for each film shown, and the wages of the technicians who show it, are always paid by the King from the Privy Purse, just as he always pays for seats in the theatre.

The Duchess in academic robes after receiving an honorary degree.

The Duke on one of his factory visits. He watches a Liverpool girl at work.

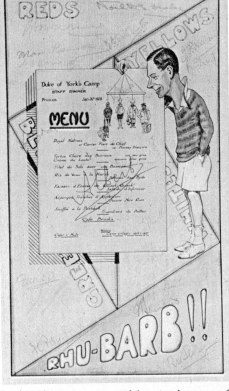

Ready for play: at his camp for public school and industrial boys.

A signed camp menu with a caricature of the "Great Chief."

A request which the King made to a newly-joined member of his official staff early in those days at 145 Piccadilly, throws considerable light on the character of the man who to-day occupies the most exalted, and perhaps the loneliest, position in the world. "Promise me you will always tell me the truth about things, even if you think I won't like it" said the Duke. A little startled by this Royal directness, the official ventured to ask if the Duke really meant what he said. The Duke assured him that he did. For many years the official worked with his Royal master on that basis, and the two were firm friends. To this day, there is nothing the King dislikes more than being put off with some half-explanation because the person concerned thinks the whole story might move the King to anger. His Majesty can be angry, as many officials and others have found out : but being told the whole truth about any happening is rarely calculated

The Duke talks to one of his campers. Informality was the key-note of the camp.

The King and Queen with the two Princesses at Abergeldie where the last of the camps was held in August 1939.

to raise his ire. It is not being told that more often makes him wrathful.

It was not a year after the Royal marriage that the first Labour Government took office under the leadership of Mr. Ramsay MacDonald. Cabinet Ministers were not among the most frequent of official callers on the King's second son, but nevertheless the Duke and Duchess of York both made it their business to become acquainted with the new men who had, something to the consternation of many older men and women, become His Majesty's Ministers, even though they had not the necessary complete majority in Parliament to give them real power. It was probably Mr. J. H. Thomas, Minister for the Colonies—the Dominions Office, now defunct itself, had not then been established—with whom the Duke had most to do. They met often and regularly on the business of the British Empire Exhibition at Wembley, and shrewd Mr. Thomas did not conceal from his political friends that he had formed a very high opinion of the character and qualifications of the Royal President. Later, in the days of the second Labour administration, it was Mr. J. R. Clynes, the former mill-boy, with whom the Duke came most closely into contact. As Home Secretary, it fell within Mr. Clynes' duty to be present in the house at the birth of Princess Margaret, in accordance with the ancient rule designed to prevent the possibility of a changeling. The Princess was born at Glamis Castle, the first scion of the Royal House to be born in Scotland for three centuries, and to Scotland Mr. Clynes had to go, to stay for two weeks as the guest of the Dowager Countess of Airlie, in nearby Airlie Castle. Small in stature, quick in mind, unbiased in judgement, Mr. Clynes became a convinced admirer of the Duke, for whose straightforwardness and conscientiousness he had the highest regard.

When the first Labour Ministers went to Buckingham Palace, to receive their Seals of Office from the hands of King George V, the very fact that most of them were crossing the Royal threshold and meeting their Sovereign in person for the first time, made for difficulties and possible misunderstandings which were averted only through understanding and goodwill on the part of the King and his new Ministers alike. They were strangers to each other, a condition not advantageous to those who must work together.

When King George VI received his first Labour Ministers, in the ninth year of his reign, conditions were very different. Many members of the new administration were old friends, with whom the King had worked throughout the war, as members of the National Government under Mr. Churchill. The Prime Minister, Mr. Attlee, himself fell into this category, as did Mr. Ernest Bevin, the Foreign Secretary. Other members of the first Labour Government with power soon found themselves on terms with the King, and it is not fanciful to suppose that his earlier experiences and contacts with the first two Labour administrations bore fruit in 1945.

Though neither the King, nor the King's sons, may, by the unwritten rules of our constitutional monarchy, show any political preferences, or take part in any public debate on matters of political controversy, there is no rule against their taking an interest in the political scene. Rather, it is part of their duty to do so. In this, the Duke of York was no less assiduous than in other matters. He frequently attended debates in the House of Lords, though he took no oral part in them. In the Commons, he was often seen, especially when Empire affairs

A young patient makes the Duke and Duchess smile during a visit to a children's hospital.

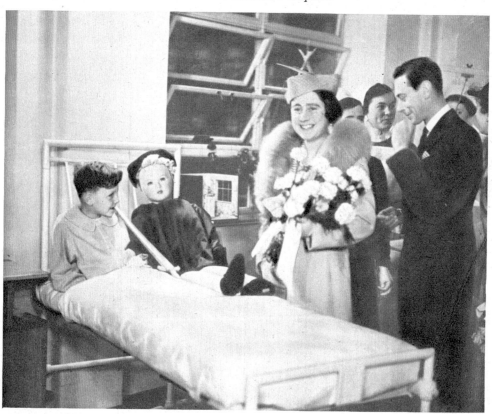

A favourite family picture with the two Princesses growing up.

were the topic of debate, sitting in the Distinguished Strangers Gallery, listening intently to the exchange of opinions below. Recently, Princess Elizabeth has given evidence that she, too, regards politics with serious attention. Two months after her marriage, she paid her first official visit to the House of Commons to hear a debate on Foreign affairs—which gave her her first opportunity of hearing a speech by Mr. Winston Churchill whom she knew so well as her father's war time Prime Minister—and let it be known that she hoped to pay many more visits in the future.

Duties took up a very great proportion of the Duke's time in the years before he came to the Throne, and his Duchess, too, was constantly busy with hospitals, charities, and other women's interests, in addition to the very active and energetic part she played in the running of her household and the upbringing of the two Princesses.

The smiling Duke and Duchess as they set out for Australia aboard H.M.S. Renown.

CHAPTER FOUR

The King who knows his Kingdoms

KING GEORGE VI is not the first British Sovereign to be King separately of each of his Dominions as well as King of England and Wales, and King of Scotland, since the Statute of Westminster which turned the Dominions into separate nations, bound only by their common allegiance to the one person who is King of each of them, was passed in the reign of his father, George V. But he is the first King of Canada to set foot on Canadian soil, and the first King of South Africa to visit the Union.

Empire matters had long held high place in the King's interests before he ever had the opportunity of visiting any of the Empire. His activities as President of the British Empire Exhibition in 1925 gave proof enough of that. In those days he made many public references to his intense desire to see for himself conditions in the King's overseas Dominions. He told the Australian and New Zealand luncheon club in London, " Travel is good for everyone. ' Go and see for yourselves ' is a fine precept if only one has the time and means to act upon it."

Since then the King has made it his business to " go and see for himself" whenever possible, with the result that he has a real first hand knowledge of local conditions in many parts of the Empire, a knowledge which enables him to understand Empire problems with more understanding and sympathy when they are put before him.

Before that first tour which took him away from London for a full six months, the Duke said that he and his Duchess were " longing to see the wonders of your countries . . . and to meet your people in their homes."

That has been the spirit of each of the other two great Empire tours, first to Canada, and then to South Africa, which the King and Queen have made since. Wherever they have gone, to remote townships hidden in the vast tracts of Canada, to isolated communities scattered in the limitless spaces of the veldt, they have talked to the people, discussed their home problems, their hopes and ambitions, so that they have left with a deep knowledge of the people of the country, as well as an experience of official ceremonial as it has been developed in the Dominions.

On their most recent tour, which took them all over the Union of South Africa, and up into the Rhodesias, as well as into the native Protectorates of Basutoland, Bechuanaland and Swaziland, it was above all this homely interest in the lives of the families which made the Royal State visit into a real tour of triumph. South Africans, of British and Boer descent alike, as

The Duchess watches the Duke enjoying a vigorous game of deck tennis on the Renown's *quarter-deck.*

well as the settlers in Northern and Southern Rhodesia, found in the King and Queen warm human beings beneath their panoply of State. And they liked what they found. The natives in the Protectorates were a little disappointed, perhaps, at the absence of gold and scarlet full dress from the King and his entourage. The plain white tropical uniform of an Admiral of the Fleet, relieved only by the blue Garter ribbon, which the King wore on all these visits, lacked something of the regal magnificence which they had expected.

But even to the natives, the presence of the King's family with the King made a special appeal. The dignity of his bearing, the measured weight of his words as he spoke to them in ceremonial terms at the great Indabas, or gatherings of tribes, made a deep impression reviving and revitalising their loyalty to the Great White King from Over the Water.

If further proof of the Royal attitude of goodwill to the coloured inhabitants of South Africa were needed, it was to be found in the delight with which the King and Queen and both Princesses listened to the haunting melody of the Bantu anthem " Xosa Sikele Afrika " with which crowds of black-skinned men, women and children greeted them everywhere as they journeyed across the Union. Aboard H.M.S. *Vanguard* on the first day of the homeward voyage, the King asked if the Marine band could play the anthem, so much did the Royal Family like it. No score of the music was aboard and so the Director of Music, Major Vivian Dunn, had to work out a score by listening to various members of the Royal Party humming what they remembered of the tune. Later, the Bantu music was played more than once as the Royal Party sat at dinner, reviving memories of eager, smiling natives welcoming their King and Queen.

Altogether the King and Queen have travelled well over 70,000 miles on journeys of State through the Empire, without taking into account their first visit to Africa when in the year after their marriage they made a private visit to East Africa for big-game hunting. Longest of their voyages up to the present has been the journey to Australia and New Zealand, which involved travelling more than 30,000 miles by sea as well as several thousand miles by land, and sailing right round the world.

After his return in July 1927, the Duke said his first impression was the wonderful loyalty of all to the Throne and Empire, loyalty in the widest sense of devotion to all those things for which the Crown and Empire stands—justice, liberty, fair play and love of peace.

" I return a thorough optimist," said the Duke. " It is impossible to despair of the future of the British race.

" The same qualities which carried us successfully through the war (of 1914-18), will I am convinced, so long as we remain united as members of one family, enable us to surmount all difficulties that may beset us however formidable or however perplexing. If we hold together we shall win through."

That same faith in the Empire was reaffirmed by the King twenty years later after the British Commonwealth had emerged from the second World War, still united, still a family, now with himself at its head.

Again at London's historic Guildhall, which had suffered much destruction from enemy bombs since he last spoke there, the King, in the longest, and one of the best, speeches of his reign, spoke of the renewed faith in the British way of life which his experiences in South Africa, whence he had just returned, had given him.

" South Africans feel most strongly that the world needs Britain now more than ever before, and there is firm faith in her ability to weather the present storms and to continue to play a noble part in shaping the future of the world " declared the King.

Then, in a peroration which he had written and phrased himself with even more care than usual, weighing every word of his sentences, the King made this declaration of faith in the destiny of our British Commonwealth of Nations.

" For myself," he said, " I share that faith. I shall hold it to the end of my days. Come what may, nothing will ever shake my belief that this old country—old in history, old in experience, old in achievement—is at heart as young and vigorous as she has ever been."

In that speech of Empire on May 15, 1947, the King paid once more high and public tribute to his wife and their daughters.

" All through the tour—and it was a long journey and often arduous —all through it," said the King, " and at every function connected with it, the Queen and our daughters were at my side to help me : and, if it achieved any success, as I know it did, that result is in large measure due to them."

The Queen and the two Princesses listened with the rest of that great and distinguished company to the King's words, and a blush of pleasure and gratitude mounted the Queen's cheeks as everyone present cheered the King's words. The King smiled warmly at his wife and at the Princesses. It was a brief moment of deep family affection and sympathy, in which the civic governors of London, the representatives of the Home Government, the High Commissioners of the Dominions, the heads of the Churches, the chiefs of the Armed Forces, and other distinguished folk who heard and watched the King, took part. It was a moment that more than any other epitomised the family feeling that the whole Empire has for the King and Queen, and told, for all the world to hear, that the Royal family of England is a united and happy one.

It was to Canada, as senior Dominion, that the honour fell of receiving the first visit by the King after his accession. The invitation came from Mr. Mackenzie King, Prime Minister of Canada, soon after the Coronation, and on Saturday May 6, 1939, the King and Queen set sail. It was seven weeks before the King and Queen returned to Britain, and during that short period of time they had written one more new chapter in the long history of the British Crown. Not only had they travelled from the East coast across the Dominion to the West and back, re-creating ties with the Mother country wherever they went, but they had also been across the border, that 3,000 miles of unguarded frontier which divides the Kingdom of Canada from the Republic of the United States, and had found at Washington and in New York a welcome just as eager, and even more vociferous, than they had received in their own Dominion.

There were no political motives attached to that brief visit to the United States. It was merely a gesture of international friendship and goodwill. But the affection which the King and Queen inspired among the American people in their short four days stay was soon to

The Duke of York opens the first session of the Federal Parliament of Australia at Canberra, the new capital.

be reflected in the heightened sympathy with which the people of the United States followed the fortunes of Britain at war.

The King, on his return, recalled that their journey had been unique historically, in that no reigning Sovereign had in time past entered one of the sister Dominions that constitute the British Empire.

" It is my earnest hope that it may also be of some importance in its influence on the Empire's future destiny," said the King.

No one accompanying the King during his wartime visits to the Canadian forces, and seeing the intense loyalty with which the men and women from that Dominion greeted him, and the pleasure with which so many recalled meeting him and the Queen in their home towns, could doubt that the King's hope was fufilled, and that that Royal visit, made in the last halcyon days of peace, did much to stimulate Canadian eagerness to stand at Britain's side.

The King's three great Empire journeys have a constitutional significance in addition to their human value. On each of them he took an active part in the affairs of the Dominion he was visiting. In Australia as the representative in person of his father, the Duke opened the new Federal Parliament House at Canberra, and opened formally the first Session of the Australian Parliament to be held within it, 26 years to the day after his father had opened the first Federal Parliament.

In Canada the King did more. In person he presided over the Canadian Parliament at Ottawa on Friday, May 19, 1939.

In exact accordance with the traditional procedure at Westminster, in the " Mother of Parliaments ", the Canadian Gentleman Usher of the Black Rod summoned members of the Canadian House of Commons

Leaving for South Africa: the Royal party at Waterloo, January 31st, 1947.

to the Bar of the Senate, just as British M.P.s are brought to the Bar of the House of Lords by Black Rod when the King opens Parliament. The only variation was the repetition of the Order to Black Rod in French—the other official language of the Dominion.

Then the King performed an historic act, assenting in person to three Bills of his Canadian Parliament, the first of them approving a trade agreement between Canada and the United States. Not since Queen Victoria attended at the House of Lords on August 12, 1854, had the Royal Assent been given by the Sovereign in person in the British Parliament, and, of course, it had never been done before in Canada.

Another act of great constitutional importance which the King carried out in Ottawa was his reception of Mr. Daniel C. Roper who presented to the King his Letters of Credence as newly appointed United States Minister to Canada—an outward symbol of the status of nationhood enjoyed by the Dominion, to which other great powers send Ministers, just as to the King's Court at St. James's. The American Minister brought a message from the President, Mr. Roosevelt, conveying the best wishes of the American people for the unqualified success of the Royal journey.

The third of the King's constitutional acts in Canada also concerned the United States, when he signed in person the Trade Treaty between the two countries.

There may not at first sight appear much significance in the fact that the King performed these acts. The Bills would have received equal validity as Acts had the Royal Assent been given as usual by Commission ; the new Minister from the United States would have carried out his functions equally well had he presented his Letters of Credence to the Governor General ; and the Trade Treaty would have had equal force had it been signed on the King's behalf. But the presence in person of the King in the Canadian Parliament brought home as nothing else could the unity of Canada with Great Britain ; the reception of their Minister by the King in person, and the signing of the Trade Treaty with them in the King's own hand, gave the American people a new feeling of kinship with Britain ; and who shall say how far the flame of closer friendship kindled then by the King and his Consort has since spread ?

In South Africa, too, the King carried out State functions. He opened in person the new Session of the Union Parliament in Cape Town, again with almost identical ceremony as at Westminster. The presence in the Parliament House at the Cape of the British Sovereign demonstrated with an emphasis otherwise impossible, that the old wounds of war were healed and that Britain and Boer had blended to produce the new grown-up nation of South Africa.

In Rhodesia, too, the King opened Parliament. Though Southern Rhodesia returns only 30 members to its House of Assembly, the same traditions, the same democratic usages were faithfully observed in that miniature Parliament, just as in the home Parliament at Westminster.

The King, when he is in his kingdoms overseas, is just as strictly observant of the Royal rule that the Sovereign takes no part in politics as he is at home. A clear example of this was given during the South African tour. Comment of an adverse kind was aroused when the Royal train passed through a certain town without stopping or slowing down. The inhabitants of that town were well known to be predominantly Nationalist and the story spread quickly that the Royal Party had passed through without a halt because they knew of this. Actually the White Train was running merely to schedule. No halt or slowing down had been arranged for at that point and the Royal passengers themselves were quite unconscious of the disappointed crowds who had gathered in the station and at the side of the line. But the King usually hears what is going on around him and it was not long before the story came to his ears. At once he realised the possible implications of the incident. With characteristic firmness he forthwith ordered a long detour in the car journey scheduled for the next day, to embrace a short visit to the town in question. So were the disappointed townsfolk satisfied, and so did the King of South Africa show that he allows himself to be affected by considerations of party politics no more than does the King of England.

In South Africa, the King and Queen and the Princesses saw many wonders, the diamond and gold mines of the Rand, the wide Zambesi River, bearing a gay-painted " Barotsi " or Royal barge, propelled by forty sweating black rowers, lions and other animals roaming at large in the great Game Reserves of the Union, the mighty wonder of the Victoria Falls, judged by many travellers as the greatest sight in the world, the Zulu impis in their ancient war-dances, the Basutos riding to the great " pitsu " or tribal gathering, and many another rare and wonderful sight whose memory will stay with them and with all who accompanied them for the rest of their lives.

These delightful experiences were intermingled with the spate of official receptions, State duties, banquets, luncheons, dances, inspections of children—Their Majesties made a point of this at every big town they visited—and other functions, public and private. There were other interludes of relaxation and pleasure, such as the days spent by the side of the Indian Ocean, at Port Elizabeth, where the White Train was " staged " in a specially built siding on the shore, to enable the Royal party and those with them to bathe from the train, an opportunity of which the King and both Princesses eagerly availed themselves. There were, too, the " braaivleis ", those open-air picnics of Boer tradition, at which all the Royal party learned to eat and enjoy the two delicacies always served on such occasions, the sasaties, which are slices of mutton, curried and cooked, and eaten from thin wooden skewers, and the boerevors, which are black meat farm sausages.

But, despite several planned " rest days ", the Royal party had practically no real freedom for complete rest and relaxation from the moment they set foot on South African soil, till they embarked again in the *Vanguard* sixty-five days later. Neither the King nor the Queen were disturbed by this : they had expected as much, and they had prepared the Princesses for it. But many South Africans felt that their Royal visitors should have had some holiday period, and there was, when the party left, a very general and sincere hope that, at some time in the future, the King and Queen and the Princesses, together or separately, will be able to return to the hospitable Union for a real holiday trip.

The Royal tour in Africa was different, in one respect, from any other Royal tour before it. For the first time, the King's Flight, under

But Munich only postponed the evil day, and when Hitler took over Czechoslovakia in March 1939, Chamberlain spoke in strong words, uttering a clear threat to the Reich. The King wrote again to him and his words show how clearly the Sovereign, from his lofty position above the arena of party politics, can form a true judgement of events.

The King wrote : "My dear Prime Minister, I feel I must send you one line to say how well I can appreciate your feelings about the recent behaviour of the German Government.

"Although this blow to your courageous efforts on behalf of peace and understanding in Europe must, I am afraid, cause you deep distress, I am sure that your labours have been anything but wasted, for they can have left no doubt in the minds of ordinary people all over the world of your love of peace, and of our readiness to discuss with any nation whatever grievance they think they have."

A world war has written itself bloodily across the pages of history since then, but the King's words, the King's summing up of Neville

Proud of her initialled bag and its coronet:
Princess Elizabeth and her sister.

77

The Silver Jubilee of King George V.   The Royal fami

Chamberlain's actions and motives, written at the time, remain true.

When at the end of September, 1940, Mr. Chamberlain was obliged by illness to resign from Mr. Churchill's Government, he wrote to the King telling of his sadness at the failure of his efforts for peace, adding " Broadly speaking, I was your first Prime Minister and I shall always recall with gratitude the confidence which you have been good enough to give me, and the increasing intimacy of your conversations which were so encouraging and helpful to me during some of the most anxious and difficult periods which have ever faced a Minister in all our long history."

Those sincere words, written within a few weeks of his death, show what Neville Chamberlain thought of his King. They are a rare tribute to the helpful part a good Sovereign plays in the task of Government.

The King was touched, as who would not be, by this letter. Replying, he paid tribute in turn to the support he had received from Mr. Chamberlain.

" I shall ever be grateful for your help and guidance during what was in many ways a very difficult period " the King wrote " for me too it will always be a pleasure to recall our many and intimate talks together.

n the balcony of Buckingham Palace, May 6th 1935.

" I have sympathised with you very much in seeing your hopes shattered by the lust and violence of a single man and yet, as I told you once before, your efforts to preserve peace were not in vain, for they established, in the eyes of the civilised world, our entire innocence of the crime which Hitler was determined to commit. For this alone, the country owes you a debt of gratitude."

With the King's approval, Mr. Winston Churchill offered his predecessor the Order of the Garter on October 1, 1940, an offer which Mr. Chamberlain declined. The offer is of special interest, as being the last occasion on which the Garter was the subject of a recommendation by the Prime Minister of the day. Subsequently the King, with the knowledge and approval of the Cabinet, took back into his own hands the bestowal of this, the highest Order of British chivalry, together with that of the Order of the Thistle. Thus it was on his own initiative that His Majesty on July 26, 1945, after receiving Mr. Churchill's resignation as Prime Minister, asked him to accept the Order of the Garter in recognition of his great services throughout the war. Mr. Churchill, however, begged His Majesty that in present circumstances he might be allowed to decline the offer.

The general story of the great events which led to the King's accession on December 11, 1936 in circumstances which he described

A document of history.   The proclamation of King George VI with the signatures of his Privy Councillors.

in his first message to Parliament as " without precedent " and at " a moment of great personal distress " are well known.   Much remains to be written when the histories of the future are compiled from the records now locked in the Royal Archives at Windsor, and from the personal papers of the leading protagonists of the time, men like the late Archbishop Lord Lang of Lambeth and the late Earl Baldwin of Bewdley.   Here are two stories of those days, never before told, which

throw an interesting light on the happenings of that historic winter's week.

When it became clear that Edward VIII was determined to lay down his Crown, and that nothing could shake him from the course on which he had resolved, it became essential for the Prime Minister of the day, who would form the main link between the reign that was ending and the new one which would follow it, to have personal contact with the Duke of York as he prepared himself to take over the dread burden of sovereignty.

But this was by no means easy to arrange. At that time only a small handful of people directly concerned knew of Edward's decision and it was vital in the public interest that the secret of the abdication should be kept until the moment when it would be made public in the proper constitutional manner by the Prime Minister's announcement in the House of Commons. Outside 145 Piccadilly the constant vigil kept by newspaper men and photographers rendered it impossible for the Prime Minister to go and see the Duke without attracting the maximum of public attention.

Similar considerations applied if the Duke went to 10 Downing Street, where at times of crisis a constant watch is always kept by newspaperdom.

But the Duke *did* see the Prime Minister on three separate occasions in the days immediately preceding his accession, yet, so skilfully were the arrangements made, no word of their meetings got into the newspapers. It was the Duke who went to No. 10. The newsmen and photographers outside did not see him arrive, even those more knowing ones who kept an eye on the garden gate of No. 10, which opens onto the Horse Guards Parade. It was at this entrance that the Duke arrived. Explanation of the pressmen's failure to note his arrival is simple. Instead of driving in his own black saloon car, easily recognisable by the silver model of a lion on the radiator, the Duke came from 145 Piccadilly in a private car belonging to a

Garter King of Arms proclaims the new King.

member of his staff who drove him down. The Duke returned home in the same way, and no one was any the wiser.

When the final decision had been taken, and the Duke knew that he was to be King, one problem remained—by which name he should be known as King. Before he was created Duke of York he had been known as Prince Albert, and Albert remained his signature as Duke,

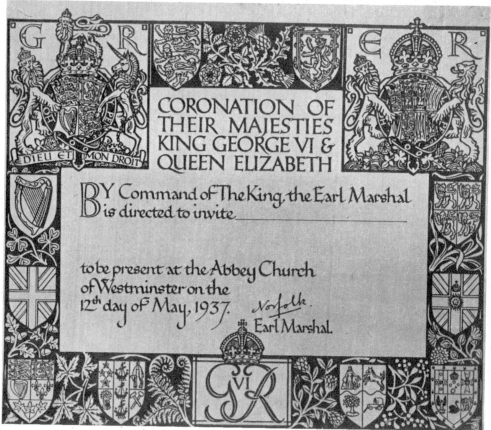

CORONATION OF
THEIR MAJESTIES
KING GEORGE VI &
QUEEN ELIZABETH

BY Command of The King, the Earl Marshal is directed to invite _____

to be present at the Abbey Church of Westminster on the 12th day of May, 1937. Norfolk. Earl Marshal.

The most eagerly sought of all invitations: to the Coronation in 1937.

while in the Royal Family circle he was known, as he continues to be known to-day, as " Bertie ".

For various reasons he did not wish to ascend the Throne as King Albert the First. For one thing, the name Albert was too much associated in the minds of the Royal Family with the Prince Consort, Queen Victoria's husband, and for another King Edward VII had dropped it from his title.

The newly-crowned King receives homage at the Abbey.

Various guesses have been made as to how he came to choose his fourth and last name, George, as his Royal style. It can be stated here with complete authority that it was the King's own personal, unhampered choice. A happier one could not have been made. In the reign of King George the Sixth, the Throne has gathered round it in increasing measure the same love, affection, and confidence, the same aura of uprightness as invested it under the wise guidance of George the Fifth, whose simple faith his son and successor so fully shares.

Graphologists of the future, comparing the similarity of character between the two monarchs, may well find material of interest in the comparison of the sign-manuals of the two Sovereigns. The similarity of the signatures is striking, so striking that the King himself used to joke, in the early days of his reign, that future historians might have difficulty in deciding whether he or his father had signed a document, until they looked at the date.

It is a coincidence that the same striking similarity exists between the handwriting of the Queen and that of Princess Elizabeth, especially in their signatures. Both start with the same clear well-defined capital E and the underlining stroke, as well as several letters, in each case have the same characteristics.

The King's sign-manual, the most important signature in the British Empire, since it gives legal authority to State documents, and imbues them with statutory powers, was changed in the eleventh year of his reign, when the setting-up of the two new Dominions of India and Pakistan in place of the old Indian Empire necessitated the dropping of the style Emperor of India from the Royal titles. Since then, the King signs himself " George R." instead of, as formerly, " George R.I."—Rex instead of Rex Imperator.

The months that followed the Silver Jubilee of King George V in May, 1935 saw much Royal history made, the death of King George V on January 20, 1936, the accession and short reign of Edward VIII, his abdication, and the accession and proclamation of the King as George VI.

Through all these momentous events which so directly and personally affected him, the King bore himself with level-headed, calm and cool confidence, supported always by the love and wisdom of his wife.

It was typical of him that in the last few days before the abdication, when members of the Royal Family withdrew for the time from the limelight of public appearances, he did not allow himself to forget his interests in industry. In his last two days as Duke of York he wrote two speeches for the Industrial Welfare Society, one for the annual general meeting in which he discussed the work of this Society, particularly

The newly-crowned Queen receives her regalia from the Archbishop.

dealing with the question of medical and surgical treatment, and the other at the Society's annual banquet. Both these speeches were read for him since he was unable to be present himself. The dinner speech was his last public utterance before becoming King.

Henceforth his words in public must always be weighed with the utmost care, as the utterances of the Sovereign. Now for the last time he could speak with the greater freedom of a Prince. In his speech the Duke spoke of the ideal, the creation of good fellowship in industry with which the Society had begun, and was proud to claim substantial progress.

To-day when the King is making a personal speech, such as his Christmas Day broadcast, he likes to introduce some human story to leaven what he is saying. So he did in his last speech as Duke. The story he told showed how deep are his human sympathies.

" I noticed in a factory once," wrote the Duke, " a small girl sitting all alone watching millions of tobacco leaves passing by on a belt. Her only job was to pick out foreign bodies such as bits of wire, nails and so on—to the onlooker a very dreary task. I said to her ' Don't you get a thrill when you find something ? '

" The little girl looked up from her work with her eyes glowing with the memory of a great event and said, ' Once I found a shilling.' "

Dickens or Barry might have imagined such an incident. The King drew it from his store of memories, told it in simple words that spoke of his knowledge of human nature.

Pomp and pageantry outside Buckingham Palace on Coronation Day.

Two days later, on December 11, the Royal Standard was broken over the " Palace With a Number " at 145 Piccadilly, and the new reign had begun. After holding his first Privy Council on December 12, at St. James's Palace, and transacting other State business the King, with the Queen and the Princesses left London for Christmas at Sandringham. When they returned to London, they said goodbye to the Piccadilly house which had been " home " for so long. They moved in to Buckingham Palace, henceforth to be their London home.

On May 12, 1937 the King and his Consort were crowned in Westminster Abbey with all the pageantry and high ceremony attaching to the consecration of the English Kings, with the recognition by the Peers and people as the Archbishop presents the King, and the taking of the Oath by the King to " govern the people of this United Kingdom of Great Britain, Ireland and the Dominions thereto belonging, according to the Statutes in Parliament agreed on, and the respective laws and custom of the same " and " to cause law and justice, in mercy, to be executed in all your judgements."

The taking of these oaths together with the Oath to maintain the Protestant Reformed Religion is a legal necessity, enjoined upon the Sovereign by the Act of Succession. The King, in accordance with ancient custom, signed an engrossed copy of the Oath, which is deposited among the records of his Court of Chancery.

He was consecrated with Holy Oil, invested with the Supertunica of Cloth of Gold, received the Golden Spurs, the Sword of State, the Pallium, or Imperial Mantle, the Orb, the Ring, the Sceptres with the Cross and Dove, and finally the Crown of St. Edward, the ancient Crown of England which is used at no other ceremony.

The Groom of the Robes is a court official who takes a central part in the Coronation ceremony. Throughout the ceremony he remains closest of all the court officials to the King's side.

With his characteristic kindly thoughtfulness, the King appointed as his Groom of the Robes, Commander (now Captain Sir) Harold Campbell, R.N., who had long been on his staff as Duke of York, and who is still Equerry to the King. Thus the man who had worked so conscientiously and long with him as assistant secretary and secretary was rewarded.

The Queen, too, was crowned, anointed with oil, while four peeresses held a canopy of Cloth of Gold over her. The Archbishop of Canterbury put on her fourth finger the Queen's Ring, and then set on her head her Crown after which Princess Elizabeth and Princess

The King with his Empire Premiers.   Left to right.   Mr. M. J. Savage, New Zealand;
Mr. J. A. Lyons, Australia; Mr. Baldwin; the King; Mr. Mackenzie King, Canada;
and General Hertzog, South Africa.

Margaret put on the specially made coronets of gold which they wore that day for the first and only time in their lives.

From the Abbey through mile after mile of cheering crowds the King and Queen drove by a long route to Buckingham Palace.

When the Queen was asked how she felt after the emotional disturbances and moving experiences of the day, she confessed that on her return to the Palace she had found the Crown a little heavy.

Never since have either the King or Queen shown any sign that they find the weight of their Crowns too heavy.   They wear them supported by their people's love.

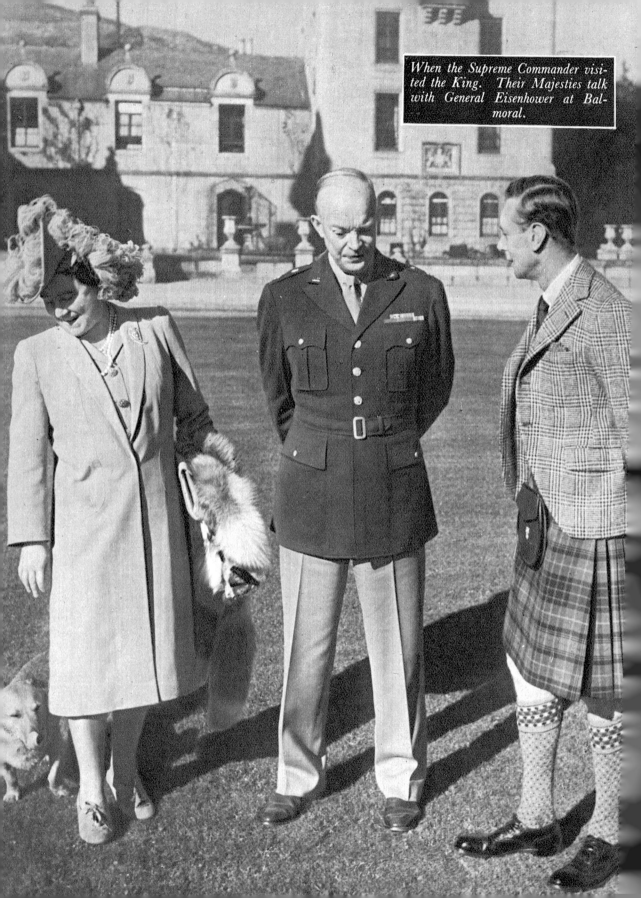

When the Supreme Commander visited the King. Their Majesties talk with General Eisenhower at Balmoral.

CHAPTER SIX

The King at War: with the Queen at his Side

THROUGHOUT the six years of war, the King and Queen remained in the midst of their subjects, taking part and sharing with them in all the ordeals of total war. They underwent the difficulties of food and clothes rationing, they spent nights in the air raid shelter with which their home, though it was Buckingham Palace, had to be equipped just like millions of other homes in London, they had the frightening and all too common experience of having their home bombed ; and, beyond all this, they took, as no one else, no leader of the Church, no high service chief, no Cabinet Minister, not even Mr. Winston Churchill himself, could take, a leading part in all the vast fields of endeavour whose one purpose was victory.

They were the central rallying points for the spiritual hopes of the whole nation, the Dominions and the rest of the Empire. Those who were privileged to work closely with the King in those terrible but vital days, those who met him and the Queen as they went about the country bringing encouragement and solace wherever they went, all tell the same story of their fortitude and their never failing confidence. Wherever the King went, to see the Prime Minister at No. 10 Downing Street, to watch progress reports of a naval battle in the underground operations room of the Admiralty, to inspect his troops in the battle-line, to talk with Air Force chiefs at their various headquarters, or to watch humble men and women workers at the factory benches, he brought always with him a sense of unity and set purpose, so that his familiar slim figure in the uniform of one or other of his three fighting services became for all the very embodiment of that dogged spirit of victory that persisted even in the darkest days after Dunkirk.

King George VI, whose reign was fated to embrace the first total war in history, saw and experienced more varied kinds of actual warfare than had any of his ancestors, even including those ancient Kings who won and held their Crowns by prowess on the battle-field. He went among his airmen to watch them taking off for raids on Germany ; he was at their air stations to welcome them back after offensive flights over enemy and enemy-occupied countries ;

he sat at lunch in the officers' mess of one bomber station in Norfolk, on a visit with the Queen, when a German raider bombed up the station—to the great alarm of the high officers of the R.A.F. sitting with the King. He visited his Navy, sleeping aboard the Home Fleet flagship in Scapa Flow ; he sailed in one of his own cruisers for France, just after D-Day, and returned from Ostend in one of his destroyers soon after the Belgian port had been liberated ; and he examined, with the eye of an expert, the Navy's new weapons for defence and offence at the naval shore establishments. He inspected hundreds of units of the Army, in many greatly different stages of war-like readiness, first the eager troops of the little British Expeditionary Force who sailed, so full of hope and confidence, to France in September 1939 ; then the sad remnants of that same force, who had lost almost everything save their spirit and their discipline, when they came back after Dunkirk ; and finally the new army, the Army of Liberation with all its splendid equipment of modern weapons, its parachutists and glider troops, as it got ready for the final assault on Germany.

To be in the firing line was an experience which most of the King's subjects in the United Kingdom involuntarily shared, since enemy bombers in modern wars take no heed of fighting fronts. But for the King this was not enough. He wished to see his forces actually engaging the enemy, and in these matters the King has a way of doing what he wishes. In all he paid five visits to the battle zones, beginning with the sober experience of an inspection of the Maginot Line, before serious battle had been joined, and ending with a much more thrilling visit to the Advanced Headquarters of General (now Field Marshal Lord) Montgomery in the Eindhoven Corridor, with the German guns emplaced less than five miles on either side of the caravan where the King slept. Of all these visits, which included a trip by air to North Africa and a visit to the British Army under Field Marshal Alexander in Italy, the King's journey to Normandy

The King greets a poilu during his visit to the Maginot Line, 1939.

on " D Plus 10 "—ten days after Allied troops had set foot again on French soil—was the most dramatic, was imbued with the greatest sense of history.

In great secrecy the King left London in the evening of June 15 by special train. He spent the night in the train on a siding at the quiet little station of Horsley in Surrey, and in the morning embarked at Portsmouth in the smart cruiser H.M.S. *Arethusa*. On her bridge, with a cluster of high ranking officers of the three Services, the King watched the scene in the busy Channel, where the life-line of the Allied invasion of Hitler's fortress of Europe stretched, in the form of a double line of shipping of almost every kind, unbroken from the shores of England to those of France.

It was a sight such as no other monarch of England, not even Edward III or Henry V whose troops invaded France with such different purpose, had seen ; and such a sight as may never be seen again. The King with his naval eye absorbed it all. He asked hundreds of questions about mines and submarine attacks, about the enemy's E-boat activities, about the flow of troops and supplies, about the state of the " Mulberries "—those artificial harbours which played so vital a role in the Allied landing, and which were then among the highest of top secrets.

At the King's order the Royal Standard was broken aboard *Arethusa* as she was passing through the convoys and minesweepers. Cheers from their crews came across the water as they realized their King was with them.

On the Normandy beaches soldiers looked up from their various tasks with a gasp of astonishment as they saw one of the ungainly amphibians known as " Ducks " drive slowly past, flying the Royal Standard of England on its radiator, and realised that their King had come to visit them. The cheers that went up in the still summer air from those pioneers of victory were among the most heartfelt that have ever greeted the King.

With little ceremony the King drove forward to where General Montgomery, Commanding the 21st Army Group, had set up his quarters in a French chateau. The thunder of guns from a cruiser, firing a supporting barrage, came to the King's ears as he bent over large scale maps with the General, while " Monty " explained his plan of campaign and outlined the tactical situation. A few hours later and the King was afloat again heading back to England.

It was on this return voyage that the King saw the first of the flying bombs. When *Arethusa* was not many miles away from Portsmouth,

A scene that was unhappily too frequent. Their Majesties inspect the ruins after an air raid.

there was a sudden alert. An unidentified aircraft had been picked up on the radar screen. In that ship there was as may well be imagined perhaps a greater degree of fighting alertness than in any other of the King's ships afloat that day, for every officer and man aboard was conscious of the great responsibility they bore for the safety of the Sovereign. A.A. guns, loaded and ready, swung questingly round and there was an atmosphere of great tension for no one quite knew what had gone wrong or how the enemy had penetrated the air defences. Suddenly across the sky a small black object flashed at such a speed that the A.A. gunners, quick as they were, could not bring it within their sights. It was all over in a moment, the alert ended, and officers and men breathed with relief, while the King went into the Captain's cabin to talk over the incident. He himself was one of the few people aboard the cruiser who knew what had happened. Before he left for

Normandy he had had from the Cabinet full accounts of the very first of the pilotless flying missiles which had landed in England, and which were, as far as the general public were concerned, still shrouded in secrecy. Now he had seen one, his first glimpse of the new impersonal war of the air.

Nor was that the only risk which the King ran at enemy hands that day. The course of the *Arethusa* across Channel and back had been most carefully plotted. Minesweepers had been purposefully busy over every yard of the water beforehand. But things at sea do not always go exactly according to plan, and at one stage at least of the outward journey there was some apprehension aboard about the danger of a floating mine of the latest type which an ingenious enemy could devise.

The King recalled the memorable incidents of that adventurous day three and a half years later in the peaceful atmosphere of Broadcasting House, after seeing a performance of " Itma ". The link between the two experiences was not obvious even to those with the King in the B.B.C. concert hall. It was in the person of Mr. Michael Standing, B.B.C. Director of Varieties, who as an R.N.V.R. officer had been on the bridge of the *Arethusa* with the King. The two talked over the historic trip in the intervals of discussing the merits of B.B.C. light entertainment.

As a footnote to the King's day in Normandy, it may be added that, owing to an unfortunate " leak " of the names of two of the villages through which the Royal party passed, General Montgomery had perforce to move his headquarters on the following night, as a precaution lest the enemy should have obtained a " fix " on its position.

Like the wives of so many thousands of the King's fighting men, the Queen could not share these experiences with her husband. Much of their ways had, by military necessity, to lie apart during the war. There were vital war secrets, momentous decisions concerning future operations, details of American aid and many other matters of

When their own home was bombed. The King and Queen inspecting the wreckage at Buckingham Palace.

The King with his Cabinet and Chiefs of Staff at Buckingham Palace.

the highest importance, which had to be known to the King, but knowledge of which he could share with no other person, not even the Queen. For example, when Mr. Churchill, in order to save the King's time as well as his own made it his practice, at the King's suggestion, to lunch every Tuesday at Buckingham Palace, the Queen did not lunch with her husband and his Prime Minister. The two, restricting themselves to a cold meal to dispense with the presence of servants, spent the time discussing fully and frankly the latest developments in war strategy, and many were the secrets exchanged between the Sovereign and the First Minister at those quiet informal luncheons.

It was at Buckingham Palace, indeed, that Mr. Churchill heard first news of that battle which he himself has described as one of the turning points of the great struggle. One evening while the Prime Minister was dining with the King and Queen he was called away from the dinner table to answer a priority telephone call.

He took the call alone in one of the secretarial offices in the Palace. He came out, his face wreathed in smiles, gaily humming under his breath " Roll out the barrel "—that then popular song of celebration. The telephone message had told him that General Montgomery and his 8th Army had attacked Field Marshal von Rommel, and the Battle of El Alamein had begun.

In many other directions, the King and Queen shared their war time lives to the full. After his first visit to a badly bombed area, when the King walked through the still smouldering rubble of Coventry, with several unexploded landmines hidden in the debris of wrecked houses, the Queen accompanied him on all the many visits he made in the wake of the German bombers. These visits wrote a new chapter in the history of British Royalty. Disregarding the often present risks of unexploded bombs or falling masonry, the King and Queen went, guarded only by two men from Scotland Yard, among their stricken people. To follow them on such visits, in the East End of London, in the suburbs and in provincial towns, was a profoundly moving experience. Men and women whose homes had been shattered, whose families had been killed by the bombs of the King's enemies, gathered round their King and Queen to tell them what they had gone through.

The King inspects his own Home Guard, the Buckingham Palace Company.

And from those least formal of Royal audiences, conducted usually against a background of broken walls, tumbling roofs and charred timbers, with gaping holes in the roadway at the King's feet, the survivors of the bombing seemed to gain a definite spiritual refreshment. Mr. Herbert Morrison, as Minister of Home Security, accompanied the King and Queen on many of these tours, and that astute politician, well versed in the art of weighing up public reaction, declared more than once that their Majesties' visits had done more to keep up the people's spirits than any other single factor. More than once the King and Queen carried with them as they walked through bomb stricken areas, the

The King and Queen interested in a paratrooper's equipment.

knowledge that their own home had been bombed. On one occasion at least, they set off from Buckingham Palace a few minutes after bombs had fallen on the Palace, before they themselves knew the extent of the damage. But they never allowed their private feelings to obtrude. None of the pitiful homeless victims of the last night's raid could guess from the demeanour of the King or Queen that they themselves were fellow sufferers.

In all Buckingham Palace and its precincts were bombed nine times, including damage by flying bomb and rocket. On several occasions the King and Queen were away, either on provincial tours, or at Windsor Castle where, when the bombing of London reached its height, they, on Cabinet advice, spent most nights. It was fortunate indeed that they were away when a German bomb fell on the Palace lawn one night a few yards from the West face of the buildings. A fragment of this bomb hurtled through one of the Palace windows, cut a neat circle of glass from the middle of a dressing table mirror, tore through the doors of a wardrobe, and embedded itself several inches deep in the wall beyond. The damaged

The King and Queen take their daughters on a wartime visit to Canadian forces in England.

*On one of the many visits to a
Service club.*

room was that on the ground floor used throughout the war by the King as his bedroom.

On Friday, September 13, 1940 there was a direct attack on Buckingham Palace by a German aircraft. The following account of this incident is by an eye-witness.

The King and Queen had just arrived in the morning at Buckingham Palace from Windsor and were in the King's little sitting-room overlooking the Palace quadrangle. Suddenly they heard the drone of an aircraft and before Their Majesties could take cover a stick of five bombs fell.

Three crashed in the quadrangle, one on the private Royal Chapel and the other in the garden. The King and Queen actually saw the bombs falling.

Again the King and Queen made a tour of inspection of a bombed area, this time with their personal feelings deeply concerned, for the men and women shaken and injured by the explosion were their own servants. Later when they inspected the wreck of the chapel, it was found to the King's great pleasure that the family Bible belonging to Queen Victoria in which his own and all other Royal births are recorded was undamaged.

Bomb damage to the Palace buildings by this and other raids was greater than was generally realised at the time, and in February 1948, nearly four years after the last of the German bombs had fallen on London, repairs to the Palace were still far from complete. This was partly due to the King's ruling that in view of the shortage of building materials and labour, special priority should not be given to any except essential repair work at the Palace. But it was also due in part to the fact that the full extent of some damage was only found at the war's end. Bombs which fell across the forecourt, for example, apparently did little damage beyond blowing out all the windows—quite a minor happening for those days. Actually the bombs damaged the structure of the Palace balcony over the central archway.

When preparations were being made for the wedding of Princess

Elizabeth, it was found that the balcony was badly cracked. Men from the Office of Works were hastily summoned. They erected a scaffolding under the balcony, completely blocking the archway beneath. This nearly resulted in Hitler's bombs having a long distance effect on the Princess's wedding, for as long as the scaffolding was there, the archway could not be used, and Royal processions would have to enter and leave by the side arches. But the men from the Office of Works decided not to allow this to happen, and before the wedding day, the balcony had been made safe, the scaffolding removed and the Princess, like other Royal brides before her, drove through the centre archway out into the forecourt.

Mr. Churchill says good-bye after Their Majesties have visited No. 10.

A common bond that united victims of the German bombing was the exchange of " bomb stories ". Men vied with each other about the extent of damage their houses had suffered. The King, too, had a bomb story of his own but, fortunately or unfortunately, he had no need to exaggerate. His house was completely demolished by a bomb. It was his former home at 145 Piccadilly which was wrecked, and the King, though sad at any destruction of property, none the less found a certain satisfaction in being able to counter stories that other people told him about their bombs with the statement " My house is completely flat ".

But bombs and bombing formed only one part, albeit a great and horrifying part, of the whole war picture, and the Queen made it her business to give aid and support to the King and to his people in many other fields of war-time activity. With her gift for correctly interpreting public feeling, the Queen took her place as a war wife, undertaking the task, harassing even for one in her privileged position, of running the King's home smoothly for him throughout the war years.

She refused steadfastly to wear uniform, though she was equally entitled to don that of the W.R.N.S., the A.T.S. or the W.A.A.F.,

The King inspects fighter pilots.

since she was Commandant-in-Chief of each of the three Women's Auxiliaries. But she felt that her place was her home, her duty to set an example to the millions of housewives who played such a thankless and difficult role in keeping their homes together. Though Her Majesty could not, as so many women did, combine her home-keeping with active war work in a factory, there can be no question that she did a tremendous service of active contribution on the women's side by her presence with the King on so many hundreds of his visits to war factories and centres of production throughout the country. She did active work in another way as well—the list of all those whom her Majesty received, in official audience and privately, during the war would embrace most of the famous war names, and many hundreds of others less well known. The heads of the three women's services, the Dowager Lady Reading, head of the W.V.S., for whose work the Queen had such deep admiration, wives of foreign Ambassadors whose countries were under the heel of the invader, distinguished visitors from America—Mrs. Roosevelt, chief among these—and the organisers of scores of schemes to help the fighting men and the civilians they had left behind, all these and many others were received by the Queen, questioned by her, and sent away happier and more confident for their contact with that gracious kindly personality.

It is part of the routine duty of an Ambassador to keep himself informed about the personalities of the Sovereign and his consort to whose court he is accredited. The opinion of the representatives of foreign powers who came into close contact with the King and Queen in the war years has therefore the special value of an expert professional judgement. However much Ambassadors and Ministers may have disagreed about other aspects of the war effort, there was never anything but unanimous agreement among them about the value of the work the King and Queen did. None of them had anything but praise for the way in which they did it. Mr. John Winant, that

" Monty " explains his tactics. The King in the Field Marshal's map-room in the Eindhoven Corridor 1944.

brilliant man of wide and deep human sympathies who represented the United States at the Court of St. James's for so much of the war, went on record, in the book he wrote just before his lamented death, in praise of the general spirit of the British people. Constantly he cites in this connection the splendid example set by the King and Queen, and expresses his own great admiration for the duty they performed.

One war-time experience which befell the Queen gave her particular pleasure. At the King's initiative, a system of weekly investitures at Buckingham Palace had been in operation since the early days of the fighting. These ceremonies were something new in Royal procedure. Not only the men—and women—who had won medals and decorations came to receive them from their Sovereign, but each recipient was allowed to bring two visitors, which meant that a total of well over 100,000 of the King's subjects had, most of them for the first time in their lives, a front seat at a ceremony of State carried out by the King himself in his Palace.

When the King went to North Africa, to visit the victorious Allied Forces there in 1943, the Queen, who was one of the Councillors of State (Princess Elizabeth was another) · to whom the King had transferred his Royal powers for the time being, held an investiture at

A Knighthood in the Field. The King dubs Lieutenant-General Sir Miles Dempsey in 21st Army Group's battle area.

the Palace in his stead. Two hundred and fifty-five officers and men received awards from her, and it is on record that this investiture took considerably longer than most, because of the Queen's interest in each recipient to whom she gave a medal. Among these was a tall colonel of a famous regiment, who received the Order of the British Empire (Military Division). A year or more later the same officer, now promoted to Brigadier, paid another visit to Buckingham Palace, this time to be made a Commander of the same Order. Officials asked him, in accordance with custom, to return the insignia of the lesser class of his Order. But the Brigadier bluntly refused. " Her Majesty the Queen gave me that decoration," he told the officials, " and no one is going to take it from me." A diplomatic way out of the impasse was found by the Brigadier accepting a suggestion that he had " lost " the insignia in question.

In addition to her other duties, the Queen took on the provision of knitted comforts for the Forces and with her orderly mind, set aside one afternoon a week for a knitting and sewing party at Buckingham Palace to which wives of officials, friends of the Queen, and Palace servants came to sit with the Queen and knit with her. No special marks were put on the garments made by the Queen herself lest their sentimental value should cause them to go astray.

Another most important responsibility which fell upon the King and Queen in the midst of their wider preoccupations was that of the upbringing of Princess Elizabeth and Princess Margaret. Their first difficult decision was on the question of whether the Princesses should be evacuated to Canada or elsewhere overseas. But as everyone knows now, the Princesses remained in this country, spending most of the war years in the comparative safety of Windsor, though, in that grim summer of 1940 when invasion seemed inevitable, plans were made for their rapid departure from England should there be risk of their falling into enemy hands.

This risk of enemy parachutists holding up and perhaps taking prisoner the King or Queen or any other member of the Royal Family was constantly present in the mind of the War Cabinet and those responsible directly for the Royal safety. The King himself carried a Sten gun in a despatch case ready at hand wherever he went by car, and his chauffeur, who had undergone full training in the Royal Horse Guards, was armed, as was the Scotland Yard detective who accompanied the King on all his travels. The Queen and the other Royal ladies also had rifle and revolver instruction. The King, perhaps to his own secret regret, never had the opportunity of using

The King with President Truman aboard H.M.S. Renown at Plymouth, August 2nd, 1945.

arms against the enemy. Had the circumstances arisen, there is little doubt he would have given good account of himself, for he is an excellent revolver shot, and, with his customary thoroughness, he kept himself in form by regular weekly target practice in the grounds of Buckingham Palace.

The King and Queen with Princess [Eliza]beth follow the Archbishop in proce[ssion to] Canterbury Cathedral to give thanks [for its] preservation.

CHAPTER SEVEN

Post-War Leadership: King and Queen and People

IN the post-war world, with all its problems and perplexities, with its doubts of the future, the King and Queen have continued to play the same part as they did during the war days. Amid the storms of political controversy, while a change in the economic structure of Great Britain, so deep and far reaching as to amount almost to a silent and bloodless revolution has been taking place, while the very form of his own Empire has altered dramatically, the King, with his Queen, has remained above and apart from all changes, the lasting symbol of the united strength of the British Commonwealth.

In many ways, great and small, the King and Queen have shown their understanding of the changed world since the war. Austerity and the need for dollar economy have their effects at Buckingham Palace as in other humbler households. The pattern of Royal events must continue, but the events themselves have been modified by the King and Queen to correspond with the spirit of the time. No longer, when clothes are rationed, the use of private cars restricted, and manpower is in short supply, would it be proper to hold evening courts at Buckingham Palace, with their call for bejewelled dresses, for big limousines with chauffeurs and footmen. But the social side of Royal activities must be kept up, even though magnificence and ornate display are concepts of the past. So at Buckingham Palace a new idea for the presentation of young women to their Majesties was evolved, and since the war the King and Queen have held afternoon outdoor " Presentation Parties " distinguishable from the larger annual Palace Garden Party only by the restriction of invitations, and because attendance ranks as presentation at Court. This solution to the twin problem of providing an opportunity for the younger generation to meet the King and Queen formally, and yet of avoiding the elaborate and expensive pageantry associated with such events in pre-war days is typical of the attitude with which the King and Queen approach all such matters.

In some quarters the question may be raised whether such formalities are necessary at all. The answer to this must depend upon the general wish of the nation, and since the King and Queen

A DUKW goes by. The King taking the salute at the Victory Parade. Mr. Attlee, Mr. Churchill, Mr. Mackenzie King and Field Marshal Smuts are at the right.

head the social life of the nation, as well as leading it in other ways, it would seem that the existence of a Court carries with it a demand for formal entry into its confines.

Though women have been deprived of the opportunities of making their curtseys to the King and Queen amid the formal splendours of a Court night at Buckingham Palace, they are still more fortunate than men in the post-war world. The King has not yet revived the Royal Levées at St. James's Palace which, in pre-war days, were the male counterpart of the Courts. Nor is there any indication of a revival of these functions, any more than there is of the reappearance of a full scale Court.

The sombre, realistic attitude of the British people towards reconstruction in a war wrecked world has been reflected both in the activities and in the speeches of the King and Queen. When the plans for the rebuilding of London were shown at County Hall by the L.C.C., there were no more interested visitors, none who asked more searching and pertinent questions about the housing of the people than the King and Queen. And so it has been with other less ambitious plans for rebuilding, all of which have had the close attention of the King and Queen.

On their visits about the country, first in the series of victory tours, which embraced visits to the Channel Islands, liberated from the German occupation, and to the Isle of Man, and in subsequent tours designed to take them into parts of the country where they had not been before, the King and Queen had as their first thought the question of reconstruction and of the resettlement in industry of the men from the Forces. When they went to the Duchy of Cornwall—the King's own property in the absence of a Duke—it was the new technique of building pre-cast houses from concrete made with the waste sand from the china-clay pits which interested them most. Not content with seeing a model house, and hearing the technical side of the building processes explained, the King and Queen asked to see one of the houses already erected. They went inside, and the Queen, with the practical knowledge of one who runs a home, examined the rooms, and the fittings, and passed approving judgement on them.

" Pre-fabs ", those temporary houses whose unattractive exteriors and ugly name conceal a great deal of comfort, are a feature of post-war Britain. The Queen, who regards it as her duty to know the living conditions of the people, has been inside several of these dwellings, has admired, as any one must who has been invited to enter them, the ingenuity and skill with which the husbands and wives have made their houselets into comfortable homes, surrounded by small but carefully tended gardens. Inspecting one of a group set up on a badly bombed site in London the Queen was surprised to find dwarf apple trees growing in the garden. The railway worker who, with his wife and children, lives in it told the Queen with pride of the magnificent harvest of many scores of pounds of apples he had garnered that summer, and the Queen was delighted at this gleam of country life illumining the dark crowded streets of a London suburb.

In the matter of rebuilding and reconstructing their own bomb-damaged home the King and Queen set, as always, an example to their people. Top priority for repairs to Buckingham Palace would have been easy to obtain. Indeed, anything less would have been un-thinkable to the Court of Queen Victoria's day. But King George VI and his Queen have given the world a new idea of Royal privileges and leadership, and the King himself gave orders that priority was only to be given to the really essential Palace repairs. The others could wait their turn until the more pressing needs of humbler homes had been met. Thus it was that the Garden Entrace to the Palace, the gateway used only by members of the Royal Family themselves, wrecked by a bomb in 1941, was not restored until three full years after the war had ended. Such minor matters as new paint on the Palace walls, untouched since 1939, too, had to wait, and the great State Rooms, all of which were cleared of their valuable furniture and paintings during the war, stood empty and desolate until not long before the engagement of Princess Elizabeth was announced. This was the signal for the restoration of some state to the Palace, to make it a fitting setting for the celebrations of the wedding of the Heiress of Britain. Rose crystal chandeliers were re-hung, deep-pile carpets re-laid, furniture brought out from its places of safety, china put back into the glass cases and pictures re-hung. The Queen herself took a personal part in this work, and the whole of the paintings in the Royal collection at the Palace were re-distributed under her supervision among the rooms and corridors to display them to better effect. In the green-carpeted long Picture Gallery, on the first floor, for example, the number of paintings was, at the Queen's order, reduced from something like one hundred and twenty to under fifty, giving each room to be seen.

These things, important in their sphere, are small compared with other matters in which the King and Queen have given, since the war's end, a lead to the nation. Foremost of all is the great question of the nation's, indeed of the world's spiritual recuperation.

Both the King and Queen are of a deeply sincere religious nature. They have watched with grateful hearts the re-awakening in so many quarters to the importance of faith and of the things of the spirit; they have been, and are still, gravely concerned at the sad lack of faith in so many others. As Head of the Established Church, the King has, as part of his Royal duties, to deal with the affairs of the Church of England. The appointment of all Archbishops and Bishops is made by him, on the recommendation of the Prime Minister, and to this, as to all other sides of his multifarious duties, the King devotes conscientious attention. The submission of names as proposed new Bishops is, for example, no empty formality. The King knows most of the leading figures of the Church well enough to be aware of their qualifications, and if in any case he thinks himself insufficiently informed, he will call for full details to satisfy himself the choice is a good one, before ratifying the appointment. But this is merely part, though a grave and responsible part, of his State duties. In his private life, the King shows

Prince Philip (now Duke of Edinburgh) escorts the Royal party at the Romsey wedding of Lord Brabourne and the Hon. Patricia Mountbatten.

quiet devotion to matters of religion. Neither he nor the Queen miss a single Sunday morning service from one year to another save through illness. When they are in residence at Buckingham Palace, they go, since their private chapel is still unusable after its bombing, to the Chapel Royal at St. James's, or to the Chapel at Wellington Barracks, itself also badly bombed. At Royal Lodge, they attend service at the small chapel nearby in the heart of Windsor Great Park. At Sandringham, they go to the village church, and at Balmoral, worship at the little church at Crathie, a mile or two away from the Castle. The service here is, of course, according to the rites of the Church of Scotland, for north of the Tweed, His Majesty is King of Scotland. The simplicity of the Scottish form of service, here or at St. Giles Cathedral, when the Court is in residence at Holyrood, in Edinburgh, makes a deep appeal to both the King and Queen. Princess Elizabeth, herself a young woman of deep religious conviction, is also fond of the Scottish forms of service. It was the Scottish metrical psalm and its

setting, "The Lord's My Shepherd, I'll not want", and not the English version, "The Lord Is My Shepherd" that she chose for her own wedding service.

In South Africa, the King followed the same rule of worship according to the forms of the country, and, as King of South Africa, with the Queen and the two Princesses, attended service for the first time in the Dutch Reformed Church at Pretoria. On other Sundays in the Union, the Royal Family attended Church of England service.

Apart from his private devotions, the King has several times since the war led his nation in acts of prayer and thanksgiving. None of these great national days of prayer has had the deeper or more devout support of the King and Queen than that set aside for intercession for the United Nations Organisation, which they attended, with the Princesses, at St. Paul's Cathedral. As a constitutional Sovereign, the King may not give expression, ever, to any political views. But neither he, nor the Queen, makes any secret of their deep and abiding hopes that the great plan for union instead of dissent, among the nations may prove effective : and any lead they can give in

After Princess Elizabeth's wedding. The King and Queen lead the procession of foreign royalties from the Abbey.

this direction is given with heart-felt gladness. It was in his own Palace of St. James's that the King entertained the delegates to the first Assembly of the United Nations, in 1945. It was to Buckingham Palace that the King and Queen invited Mr. Marshall, Secretary of State for the United States, Mr. Molotov, Soviet Foreign Minister, M. Bidault, French Foreign Minister, and Mr. Bevin, our own Foreign Minister, and their assistants, during the abortive talks of the Foreign Ministers on the German Peace Treaty, in London. And when the UNO

The King at the salute with the Queen at his side.

Council is in session abroad, the King reads every word of the dispatches from his representatives there with the closest attention.

He knows, no one better, how much the future of our civilisation depends on peace, and how much peace may, in turn, depend on the greatest of the post-war experiments, the United Nations Organisation.

One other matter of vital concern to the future is one which engages the close and constant attention of the King and the Queen : the welfare of the younger generation. As a young man in New Zealand, in 1927, the King coined a phrase at a Government luncheon at Wellington, the capital : " Take care of the children, and the country will take care of itself ". Since then, the King has had to devote a vast proportion of his time in helping his Ministers to " take care of the country ", so that his views on the ability of a country to take care of itself may have undergone some modification. But his views about children have not. It is naturally to Princess Elizabeth, as a representative herself of the younger generation that most Royal duties concerned with young folk fall : duties which now her sister Princess Margaret is beginning to share with her. But the King and Queen themselves take the greatest possible interest in all that is done for the welfare of youth, and both officially, in public, and personally, in private, do much in many ways to help the work of those who look after the citizens of to-morrow.

CHAPTER EIGHT

Family Life at Buckingham Palace

BEHIND the grey stone front of Buckingham Palace, where the scars of the war wounds inflicted by Hitler's bombers are still plain to see, is the official residence of the King of England and his Consort. The red-carpeted corridors with their picture-hung walls lead to State rooms of beautiful proportions and upholstered magnificence, with deep carpets, ceilings encrusted with gold, and lovely period furniture that could be given place of honour in a museum. In smaller rooms the King's secretaries and officials, the members of the Queen's Household, including her Ladies in Waiting, and the clerks and typists carry on the daily official work of the Royal Household.

But the Palace is more than an official residence. It is the London home of a home-loving family. Privacy is the most treasured possession of Royal personages. To spend an hour or two in quiet relaxation in the family circle around their own fireside in the winter, or walking in the Palace gardens in spring or summer, is a rare pleasure for the King and Queen, so much of whose time must be spent among the crowds or receiving official callers. Because such times are rare, they are all the more valued, and there is nothing that gives the King and Queen more pleasure when they are in London than a quiet evening together. Until her marriage, Princess Elizabeth formed part of this family circle with her sister, and often in the evenings after dinner, the King and Queen would sit listening to her singing while Princess Margaret accompanied her at the piano. Now with Princess Elizabeth away beginning a family life of her own, there is a gap in the Palace circle, a gap which the King and Queen, like any other fond father and mother, feel keenly, happy though they are in their daughter's happiness.

Such domestic scenes, and the small dances which the King and Queen from time to time give for their daughters, represent a facet of simple family life which would, to most people outside the British Empire, seem incompatible with the demands of monarchical splendour. It is, for example, difficult to imagine Louis XIV sitting down at such a quiet family gathering. Yet, to British minds, there is nothing

After an opera visit : both the Queen and Princess Elizabeth are music lovers.

incongruous in the idea of the Sovereign, when his official business for the day is over, joining his domestic circle for relaxation. On the contrary, such a combination of the exercise of the supreme functions of government with the normal life of a family man is part, and an essential part, of the modern British idea of monarchy.

But it is not at Buckingham Palace, comfortable and free from the stilted atmosphere of State as the private Royal apartments may be, that the King and Queen enjoy family life to the full. Such pleasures are more to be found at either of the two houses that form their private residences. One is Sandringham in Norfolk, where the King likes, just as his father did before him, to lead the life of a country squire rather than that of a monarch. The other is Royal Lodge, perhaps the best loved of all the Royal residences because it, more than any other, partakes of the character of a private home. No press photographs of the Royal family are taken at Royal Lodge. No record of their activities there is made public. There, more than anywhere else, the King and Queen like to feel they are at home, and entitled, as much as any other couple in the country, to regard their home as their "castle", whose privacy may not be intruded upon save at their own invitation.

Both the King and Queen have been country lovers all their lives, and, in their early days as Duke and Duchess of York, it was a source of continual regret to them that they had no country house of their own, a state of affairs that was remedied in 1932, when King George V gave them Royal Lodge, a small house in Windsor Great Park. There, the two Princesses, then aged six years, and eighteen months respectively, could have more room to play than at their Piccadilly home. There, the Duke could join in their games without being watched by the crowds, and there, too, he could dig and plant and prune and take a generally active interest in gardening which has always been—and still is—one of his favourite hobbies.

The King and Queen and Princess Elizabeth at a service in the cloisters of Canterbury Cathedral.

An unusual picture. The King helps the Queen across an ancient stone stile in the Isle of Man.

So the house, set in green country far from the crowds, became the week-end home of the Duke and the Duchess and their family, and, when the Duke became King, it remained their retreat, the place where, above all others, they could put off the trappings of Royalty, lay aside the cares of State, and lead the ordinary lives of private people.

The Royal Lodge was built by King George IV for his own use. He lived at the Lodge in preference to Windsor Castle, as the latter was very cold and uncomfortable. It was built on a modest scale, and the Duke and Duchess of York made some additions to it when they first went there to live.

Few guests, if any, outside the immediate circle of the close friends of the King and Queen receive invitations to the Lodge. Official visitors, foreign sovereigns and emissaries, are received by the King at Windsor Castle, stay there as his guests. At Royal Lodge, the King and Queen regard themselves as private people, free, in their off-duty hours, to entertain only their private friends. Equerries and ladies-in-waiting are not in attendance, but, even here, the King can never be entirely free from the call of duty, and a private telephone line connecting the Lodge with Buckingham Palace enables him to maintain contact with his secretaries and ministers. No Court Circular is issued from the soft-pink walled house.

For the King and Queen, Royal Lodge is a haven of privacy. But it is less than an hour's drive from London, and, in the event of a suddenly arising crisis, the King can be back at the centre of affairs without loss of time.

It was at Royal Lodge that Princess Elizabeth and the Duke of Edinburgh spent their first week-ends after they had returned to London from Sandringham, where they spent their first married Christmas.

At Sandringham, much the same rules apply, and behind the high iron gates of the big estate, the King lays aside the pomp of Royalty, to live as a private country gentleman with his wife and family. Here

The Queen in a favourite robe-de-style at the L.C.C. evening reception with the King and the two Princesses on the eve of the announcement of Princess Elizabeth's engagement.

is where the Royal family invariably spend that festival that is more than any other a family festival, the festival of Christmas : and it is from his comfortable study on the ground floor here, that the King talks each year to his great family of peoples all over the world in the Christmas Day broadcast which he, following the example of his father, has made a regular and greatly appreciated feature of the nation's and the Empire's Christmas.

In his first broadcast as King from Sandringham, in Coronation Year, the King clearly indicated that he did not intend to make the broadcast an annual event. " You would not wish me to carry on unvaried a tradition so personal to my father " he said. But events of history caused that idea to be abandoned. First the perils of war, then the rejoicing of victory, brought the King to the microphone again at successive Christmases to speak to his greater family from the midst of his own family. It was the personal family touch in his Christmas Day broadcast in 1947, which touched millions of hearts all the world over when he said :

" To the Queen and myself, the past year has brought a personal

Family group at the piano. This is one of Their Majesties' favourite studies.

happiness as great as any we have ever known. Our elder daughter has wedded with our blessing the man she loves and one whom we love too.

"Our joy has been increased a thousandfold by knowing that it is so widely shared."

His peoples, listening to the voice of their King and Sovereign, heard the words of a man and a father.

Broadcasting has forged another bond between King and people in a very different manner and in a much less important sphere. In ancient days, monarchs took their pleasures in such matters as hawking, or the Court performances of the King's Players, pleasures in which their subjects could not join. To-day, the King and Queen—and their daughters—like so many thousands of other families, find one of their greatest pleasures in sitting together listening to the radio programmes that may be heard with equal clarity in Palace and in cottage. And as further proof that they share their people's tastes, the King and Queen have let it be known that their favourite radio entertainment is "Itma", that rapid-fire hotch-potch of absurdity and shrewd comment on the affairs of the day which has one of the biggest of all listening publics. It was a performance of "Itma" which the King and Queen saw when they visited Broadcasting House with Princess Margaret, to be televised from the studio for the first time. They heard a symphony concert, too, and a mystery play, and watched other activities of the BBC, but it was at "Itma" that they spent most time, and found most enjoyment.

The King and Queen told Mr. Tommy Handley, at the end of the show, that the records made when he appeared at a Command Performance at Windsor Castle were worn out, so often had they been played : and the King revealed himself as a regular "Itma" listener by telling Mr. Handley that he had been most sorry to have been forced to miss the show completely the previous week.

Several years ago, before the "Itma" show was anything like so well known, photographs of the King and Queen were being taken at Windsor Castle. It was important that they should be good, as they would be distributed through the Ministry of Information, all over the Empire and among allied countries. But, for some reason or another, nothing would go right. The photographers could not get

Where the Royal family relax : a happy group at Royal Lodge.

the King to pose as they wished and the expression on his face was anything but happy. Finally, the Queen suggested a picture of the King sitting at his desk telephoning. He sat down, picked up the receiver, and said in his deepest voice, "This is Fumf speaking,"—the "Itma" catchword of those war days—whereat everyone, including the King himself and the Queen, burst into laughter, and the photographers obtained some very happy pictures.

But, of course, Mr. Handley and his friends are by no means the only Royal radio favourites. Each of the Royal family likes listening to radio programmes connected with their own special interests. Princess Elizabeth, for example, is, like the Queen, fond of hearing a symphony concert conducted by Sir Adrian Boult, or one of the other front rank conductors, while the King's particular tastes do not run in that direction. Generally speaking, light entertainments, "Much

Binding-in-the-Marsh " among them, are greatest favourites with Royal, as with so many other, listeners.

The Queen has made a life-long interest of literature. She is deeply versed in both classical and modern fiction and *belles-lettres*, French as well as English, and counts several leading literary figures, Sir Osbert Sitwell among them, as her personal friends. To the King, who is compelled to do so much reading—and often such dull reading—in the course of his daily work, reading for pleasure is less of a change than for most of us, but His Majesty is always well abreast of modern literary development, and reads a great proportion of the more serious books that appear on world politics and problems, war history, and biography. He is no admirer of ultra-modern poetry. Kipling, that great singer of England and her virtues, whose popular appeal has shrunk very considerably in the past twenty years, is still a favourite of both the King and Queen.

On the domestic side, an innovation of the Queen's both shows that rationing is strictly observed in the Royal household, and illustrates the personal attention Her Majesty pays to matters of household routine. Ever since the days of Queen Victoria, a speciality served at the buffets on Court nights, and at other similar functions at the Palace, has been miniature mutton pies, made to a recipe handed down

The King broadcasting to the Empire from Buckingham Palace on the outbreak of war, September 3rd, 1939

in the Royal kitchens, each pie making no more than a couple of mouthfuls. When the first large scale evening functions were planned after the war, it seemed that the tradition of the mutton pies must be abandoned, for extra meat rations could certainly not be obtained for them. Then the Queen had an idea. Why not substitute venison, of which there were ample supplies in the Palace? Experimental pies were baked, tasted by the Queen, and pronounced excellent.

Of the several hundred people who have eaten and enjoyed these delicacies at Palace parties since, few know the secret of the substitution.

Rationing at Buckingham Palace is a matter on which, in some quarters, a certain amount of misunderstanding has arisen. Of course, the King and Queen and the Princesses do not have to exist entirely on their rationed foodstuffs. Their menus can be, and are, supplemented with unrationed foods, poultry, game, fish, and so on. Even though these items may be scarce in the open market, most of them are available from the King's farms at Sandringham and Windsor, from which, actually, a very large proportion of the raw materials for the Palace kitchens, as well as the fresh fruit of which the King and Queen and Princesses are particularly fond, is drawn. It is little known that, to comply with the King's wish that all his affairs shall be run on a business-like basis, all foodstuffs supplied in this way from the Royal farms are paid for from the Household budget. This sounds like taking money out of one pocket and putting it into the other, but in practice, it means that the farm and the household accounts show a true and accurate picture.

Neither the King nor the Queen, nor either of their daughters, could be described as a gourmet. Their preference is always for simple dishes, for cooking that is plain but good, and not for big meals of many courses. An illustration of this occurred early in the tour of South Africa, when, on the White Train, where the generous hearted and hospitable South African authorities had gone to great lengths to produce lavish menus, calculated both to show the resources of the Union, and to appeal to visitors from rationed Britain, the Queen after the first day or two, requested that the number of courses at each meal should be considerably curtailed, though both she and the King and the two Princesses, thoroughly enjoyed in reason the good fare that was everywhere provided.

At Buckingham Palace itself, a great change, planned by the King and Queen before the war, has recently been put into effect in the Royal kitchens, where, for the first time in memory, an Englishman holds the post of *chef-de-cuisine*. He is Mr. Ronald Aubrey, a tall,

A garden party to farmers and tenants in the grounds of Sandringham House.

clean-shaven Yorkshireman, who, before the war, was private chef to the King and Queen at Royal Lodge. Aubrey, who is a man of ideas, has had the big, old-fashioned and rather gloomy Palace kitchens remodelled to his own designs, with walls painted a gay yellow, and a battery of modern electric cookers and other electric devices to supplement the gas cookers. At the direct orders of the Queen, he is introducing more and more traditional British dishes into the Royal menus in place of the French cooking that was formerly the invariable rule in Royal kitchens.

This is but one of many instances that could be given of the way in which the Queen, in the midst of her public responsibilities and duties, devotes her attention to the all-important task of running the King's home. No better-run, certainly no happier home than his own

could be found in all the King's wide dominions. Neither would, nor could be the case were it not for the personal interest and the practical good sense of the gracious lady who is at its head. A thoroughly efficient and devoted staff is responsible, of course, for the daily routine running of the King's home, at the Palace, at Windsor Castle, Sandringham, Balmoral, or Royal Lodge. But without the constant personal interest and supervision of a wife, even the smoothest-running domestic organisation may leave something to be desired : and Her Majesty is a wife as well as a Queen. She shares with the King the characteristic of being thorough in all she does. Hence, though she naturally takes little part in the day-to-day running of the Palace beyond such matters as choosing herself each day's menus, she knows to the minutest detail how the Palace organisation works, and can check at once if where and why anything is going wrong.

Probably the best pointer to the happy relationships within the Royal family circle is to be found in the simple fact of the names by which the King and Queen and their children know each other.

The formal " Sir " and " Ma'am " by which even the highest members of their Court, men and women who have been their friends for many years, always address the King and Queen, are never used, have never been used, by Princess Elizabeth or Princess Margaret. They call their parents " Papa " and " Mummie ". Princess Elizabeth is still known in the family circle as " Lilibet ", the name she gave herself in her first babyish efforts to pronounce Elizabeth. Princess Margaret Rose—as she is christened—has always been known as " Margaret ". The Queen calls her husband " Bertie ", his family name since boyhood. The King calls his wife " Elizabeth ".

For twenty-five years now, the King and Queen have been together, a happy husband and wife, happy in each other's love and company, happy in the love and affection of their two daughters, to which has recently been added the new, attractive figure of their son-in-law, the Duke of Edinburgh, whom, as the King himself said, " We love too." In that time, they have rarely been apart save at the call of State duty. They have spent all twenty-five of their wedding anniversaries together, most quietly by themselves at home.

One, their fourteenth, they celebrated in some state at Windsor Castle, for it was Coronation Year, and four of the Ruling Princes of India, in England to do honour to the last crowned Emperor, lunched with them. Another, their twenty-fourth, they observed on the high seas, two days out of Cape Town, in the home-bound *Vanguard*.

This year, their Silver Anniversary is the occasion for Empire-wide

SILVER WEDDING

rejoicing, with a Service of Thanksgiving led by the Archbishop of Canterbury at St. Paul's, where, in the war-stricken days of 1918, thirty years ago, King George V and Queen Mary, too, went to give thanks on their own Silver Wedding.

The years since then have brought great destruction and misery on the world, have seen the shattering of many splendid hopes, and the King and Queen have shared the dangers, and the sufferings, and the disappointments of their peoples. But for them, personally, the twenty-five years since they walked out of Westminster Abbey as man and wife have been happy ones, blessed with the happiness they have brought each other. And the whole Empire prays that their happiness may continue, that the festivities and rejoicing of this Silver Year may, as anniversary succeeds anniversary, grow and mount to the splendour of the celebration of their Golden Wedding.

MADE AND PRINTED IN GREAT BRITAIN BY L. T. A. ROBINSON, LTD., LONDON, S.W.9